British Defence

Making Contemporary Britain

General Editor: Anthony Seldon
Consultant Editor: Peter Hennessy

Published

Northern Ireland since 1968
Paul Arthur and Keith Jeffery

Britain and the Suez Crisis
David Carlton

British Defence since 1945
Michael Dockrill

Britain and the Falklands War
Lawrence Freedman

Forthcoming

British Industry since 1945
Margaret Ackrill

British General Elections since 1945
David Butler

Electoral Change since 1945
Ivor Crewe

The End of Empire
John Darwin

The Attlee Government
Peter Hennessy

Political Consensus since 1945
Dennis Kavanagh and Peter Morris

Race Relations since 1945
Zig Layton-Henry

Britain and the Korean War
Callum Macdonald

Crime and Criminal Justice since 1945
Terence Morris

The Mass Media
Colin Seymour-Ure

Government and the Unions
Robert Taylor

Science and Politics
Thomas Wilkie

Terrorism
Paul Wilkinson

Institute of Contemporary British History
34 Tavistock Square, London WC1H 9EZ

British Defence since 1945

Michael Dockrill

Basil Blackwell

Copyright © Michael Dockrill 1988

First published 1988
First published in USA 1989

Basil Blackwell Ltd
108 Cowley Road, Oxford, OX4 1JF, UK

Basil Blackwell Inc.
432 Park Avenue South, Suite 1503
New York, NY 10016, USA

All rights reserved. Except for the quotation of short passages for the purposes of criticism and review, no part of this publication may be reproduced, stored in a retrieval system, or transmitted, in any form or by any means, electronic, mechanical, photocopying, recording or otherwise, without the prior permission of the publisher.

Except in the United States of America, this book is sold subject to the condition that it shall not, by way of trade or otherwise, be lent, re-sold, hired out, or otherwise circulated without the publisher's prior consent in any form of binding or cover other than that in which it is published and without a similar condition including this condition being imposed on the subsequent purchaser.

British Library Cataloguing in Publication Data

Dockrill, Michael L. (Michael Lawrence), *1936–*
  British defence since 1945.
  1. Great Britain. Defence. Policies of government, 1945-1988
  I. Title
  355′.0335′41
  ISBN 0-631-16054-X
  ISBN 0-631-16055-8 Pbk

Library of Congress Cataloging in Publication Data

Dockrill, M. L. (Michael L.)
  British defence since 1945.
  (Making contemporary Britain)
  Bibliography: p.
  Includes index.
  1. Great Britain–Military policy. 2. Great Britain–Armed Forces–History–20th century. 3. Great Britain–History, Military–20th century. I. Title. II. Series.
  UA647.D72   1988   355′.0335′41   88-8042
  ISBN 0-631-16054-X
  ISBN 0-631-16055-8 (pbk.)

Typeset in 11 on 13pt Ehrhardt
by Joshua Associates Ltd, Oxford
Printed in Great Britain by Page Bros (Norwich) Ltd

Contents

General Editor's Preface	vi
1 Introduction	1
2 Historical Background	14
3 From the End of the Second World War to the Korean War, 1945–1950	20
4 From the Korean War to the Suez Crisis, 1950–1956	41
5 The Sandys White Paper and its Consequences, 1957–1963	65
6 The End of Britain's Role East of Suez, 1964–1968	82
7 Britain's Defence Problems in the 1970s	99
8 The Thatcher Government and Defence, 1979–1988	111
9 Conclusion	125
Appendix I Future Defence Policy: Report by the Chiefs of Staff, 22 May 1947	132
Appendix II Defence: Outline of Future Policy, 1957	139
Appendix III Supplementary Statement on Defence Policy, 1967	146
Appendix IV United Kingdom Defence Expenditure, 1948–1979	151
Appendix V The United Kingdom Defence Programme: the Way Forward, 1981	153
Outline Chronology	158
Further Reading	164
Index	167

General Editor's Preface

The Institute of Contemporary British History's series *Making Contemporary Britain* is aimed directly at undergraduates, school students and others interested in learning more about topics in post-war British history. In the series, authors are less concerned with breaking new ground than with presenting clear and balanced overviews of the state of knowledge on each of the topics.

The ICBH was founded in October 1986 with the objective of promoting at every level the study of British history since 1945. To that end it publishes books and a quarterly journal, *Contemporary Record*; it organizes seminars and conferences for school students, undergraduates, researchers and teachers of post-war history; and it runs a number of research programmes and other activities.

A central belief of the ICBH's work is that post-war history is too often neglected in British schools, institutes of higher education and beyond. The ICBH acknowledges the validity of the arguments against the study of recent history, notably the problems of bias, of overly subjective teaching and writing, and the difficulties of perspective. But it believes that the values of studying post-war history outweigh the drawbacks, and that the health and future of a liberal democracy require that its citizens know more about the most recent past of their country than the limited knowledge possessed by British citizens, young and old, today. Indeed, the ICBH believes that the dangers of political indoctrination are higher where the young are *not* informed of the recent past.

Foreign policy since the war has been much written about,

and there are several good texts on the market. Many books have been written on specific events: Korea, Suez and the Falklands wars, as well as on nuclear weapons and policy. There is a clear need, however, for a short volume which gives an overview of *defence* policy. Michael Dockrill has provided such a book.

He begins by describing the machinery by which defence policy is made, and reveals how loose defence and foreign policy coordination has often been. Suez was a prime example of poor coordination; the Falklands War, in contrast, exhibited the benefits of both working in harmony. He also describes the gradual subordination of the priorities of the individual armed services to political and financial influences. The single most important event in this process was the creation of a unified Ministry of Defence in 1964, in the face of intense opposition from the three services.

The bulk of the book is concerned with the evolution of policy. The author gives a rapid overview of defence history from the ending of the Boer War in 1902 to the termination of the Second World War in 1945. Thereafter, he pilots the reader skilfully through the events that followed rapidly upon each other in the early post-war years: the origins of the Cold War, the formation of NATO, the Korean War and the Iranian oil crisis in the early 1950s.

It was under a Conservative government that defence expenditure was cut back in the early to mid-1950s. This was a period in which the hard economic facts of life began to pinch, and in which Britain steadily adjusted its defence and overseas policies in the light of what it could afford. In the mid to late 1960s, a Labour government, with the tenacious Denis Healey as Minister of Defence, maintained very similar defence priorities to the Conservatives. Labour in opposition often looked vulnerable to pressures which might have induced a *volte face* on defence policy, especially in relation to nuclear weapons, but in its eleven years in office after 1964, it maintained the broad defence policy consensus. After the consensus has broken down in many other areas, it looks set to continue in the defence sphere, at least until such time as a radical Labour government comes to power.

Anthony Seldon

1 Introduction

Since 1945, Britain has evolved a complex administrative and policy-making structure to organize the country's defence establishment and to plan future strategy. Despite the advent of the welfare state and the increasing preoccupation of the state with domestic issues, the defence of the realm continues to be of overriding importance to all governments, whatever their political composition. Notwithstanding the considerable organizational changes that have taken place since 1945, the Cabinet and its Defence and Overseas Policy Committee (the Defence Committee before 1963) remain at the centre of the decision-making process, with the Secretary of State for Defence as the pivotal figure.

Of course, in a democratic system the Cabinet has to take into account a wide variety of arguments and counter-arguments from inside and outside the defence establishment before making a final decision on defence and other issues. In practice, the Cabinet, meeting only once a week on average and with an overcrowded agenda, usually routinely approves policies which have already been subjected to a laborious process of examination and consultation with interested parties at departmental and ministerial level.

The Prime Minister and the Defence Secretary take the leading roles in determining the broader aspects of defence policy, although other Ministers have an important part to play. The Foreign Secretary, concerned to ensure that the country's defences are capable of providing adequate support to British diplomacy, the Chancellor of the Exchequer, preoccupied with the financial implications of defence measures, and other Ministers concerned with related employment and industrial issues, must be consulted.

As members of the ruling political party, with a majority in the House of Commons, Ministers must ensure that their parliamentary supporters are broadly in agreement with the measures the government is proposing to lay before the House. The tight discipline which the party Whips in the Commons can impose on Members of Parliament ensures that legislation is passed with the necessary majority. However, no government wants to forces its MPs to agree to measures with which they disagree and risk the humiliation of a substantially reduced majority resulting from its disgruntled backbenchers either abstaining or even voting for Opposition amendments.

The government can and does seek to limit public debate on contentious issues for as long as possible by means of the secrecy it can impose on a traditionally loyal and close-knit bureaucracy, thus inhibiting media discussion of substantive issues before they are presented to Parliament. In recent years, however, civil service sources have been more ready to 'leak' information about government proposals to the press than hitherto, thus causing embarrassing publicity about matters on which Ministers would have preferred silence. The practice of releasing so-called 'Green Papers' (consultative documents which set out the main issues and the government's case) in advance of legislation have not really satisfied those who complain of excessive secrecy, and who have accused the government of special pleading and of massaging the facts to support its case.

However, despite the government's control over the release of information, Parliament has, in recent years, developed mechanisms for extracting more details about defence issues from the Ministry of Defence than was previously possible. Before 1914, politicians left military planning strictly to the military, except where a Prime Minister like Arthur Balfour took a keen interest in strategic matters. It was often noted how the House of Commons emptied when defence debates were imminent. The government's only concern was to muster enough votes to ensure the passage of the service estimates.

Even after 1918, when public consciousness about defence had been heightened as a result of the experiences of the First World War, succeeding governments evolved their defence policies with little external interference. However, the cautious and limited rearmament programmes after 1933, which concentrated resources chiefly on the navy and the RAF, were tailored to meet the politicians' belief that the public would not stand for dramatic increases in armaments.

The most strenuous opposition to a government's defence policy usually came from elements on the left, who campaigned against what they regarded as excessive expenditure on defence, or on the right, who feared that insufficient money was being spent on national security. Thus, Winston Churchill and a small band of parliamentary supporters during the late 1930s were active in denouncing the Chamberlain government's inadequate response to the menace of National Socialist Germany. After 1945, there tended to be a consensus between the leaderships of the Labour and Conservative parties about defence and foreign policies, and protests from small sections of their respective backbenchers about these issues were usually fairly easily contained.

Unlike the United States' Congress, which has developed a network of investigative committees and sub-committees, Parliament originally had only the Public Accounts Committee and the Select Committee on Estimates. Both oversee public expenditure, and the latter issues reports on defence questions. However, neither can act until Parliament has approved the budget, and defence is only one of a large number of their concerns. In 1971 a Sub-committee on Defence and External Affairs of the Expenditure Committee was established in response to parliamentary pressure for a greater say in these important areas. In 1980 this became the more specialist Select Committee on Defence. Consisting of MPs from the main parties, the committee has performed a useful service in questioning Defence Ministers and their senior civil servants about defence policy. This has provided the public with more information about the subject, although it is doubtful whether its impact on decision-making has been very great.

Before defence legislation, White Papers and Statements on Defence Estimates come before Parliament, they are subjected to a long process of deliberation, drafting and counter-drafting in the defence establishment, followed by discussions between Ministers and finally meetings of the Defence and Overseas Policy Committee before final presentation to the Cabinet. Once Cabinet approval has been obtained, any of the armed service leaders who feel that the interests of their own service have suffered and that their representations have either been ignored or rejected can only hope that the decision will be reversed as a result of parliamentary pressure. Unlike the United States, where it is not unknown for the Joint Chiefs to provide Congressional Committees with classified information in order to discredit executive policies which are unpalatable to the armed services, the British Chiefs of Staff have tended to eschew such activities – although Winston Churchill was supplied with material on defence and foreign policies during the 1930s from Foreign Office and intelligence sources to aid him in his campaign against appeasement.

However, there are a number of MPs (often former officers) who have identified themselves with the interests of one or other of the armed services and frequently campaign against policy changes. Defence contractors, especially shipbuilders, have also acted in the past as a strong pressure group, lobbying MPs and financing campaigns against defence measures which threaten their interests. When allied to, or supported by, defence correspondents of the 'quality' newspapers, who can bring the issue before a wider audience, the influence of these groups can be formidable, although it would require a major parliamentary revolt by its supporters to force a government to make more than minor changes in its legislation.

The Chiefs of Staff Committee, established in 1923 to provide the Cabinet with advice and information about defence planning and strategic matters, is supposed to represent the interests of the services on defence questions and is usually consulted early in the legislative planning stage. However, the Committee has not had a harmonious existence since its inception. Each Chief is, of course, the head of one of the armed services and has regarded himself as its spokesman.

Given the competition between the three services for the scarce defence resources available, each of the Chiefs has asserted the importance of his own arm over the others in arguments about strategy. When, as a result, the Committee was threatened with deadlock, the Chiefs frequently resorted to a series of compromises whereby the interests of each service was upheld, thus rendering their recommendations to the government all but useless. Indeed, during the late 1930s the Chiefs, anxious to avoid a confrontation with the Chamberlain government which was determined on a policy of appeasing the Axis powers, merely supplied strategic advice which conformed with that policy.

Occasionally, a strong-minded Chief of Staff, especially one who could find his way around the Whitehall bureaucratic jungle, could persuade the government to adopt policies which were in the interests of his service. The Chief of the Air Staff in the 1920s, the redoubtable Lord Trenchard, was very skilful in getting his own way, and as a result successfully defended the RAF from absorption by the army and navy. Similarly, Lord Mountbatten, when First Sea Lord in 1957, claimed that he was able to influence the Minister of Defence, Duncan Sandys, to protect the Royal Navy from some of the worst of Sandys's proposed cuts. This is rare. Between 1947 and 1957, it is true, the Chiefs of Staff were able to frustrate any thoroughgoing reform either of the defence establishment or of the cumbrous armed services themselves, but they were supported in their opposition by powerful Ministers and vested interests in the bureaucracy, while successive Prime Ministers had neither the time nor the inclination to support their Ministers of Defence in forcing changes through.

It has been suggested that for this reason Harold Macmillan deliberately appointed relatively insignificant figures as Secretaries of War and Air and First Lord of the Admiralty in early 1957 to lessen the opposition Duncan Sandys would have to face during his reorganization of the armed services. Sir Gerald Templer, the Chief of the Imperial General Staff during this period, was a determined personality who vigorously opposed deep cuts in army strength, but he did not prevail. Sandys was the first Minister of Defence who was able to dominate the defence establishment. He achieved this as a result of the full support he received from the Prime Minister and the Chancellor of the Exchequer in his quest for substantial savings in the defence estimates. He did not consult the Chiefs of Staff in advance about his plans and completely ignored their subsequent protests.

After 1957, the powers of the Minister of Defence were gradually extended until, as a result of the 1963 White Paper, a unified Ministry of Defence was created, with the former Secretaries of State for the individual services reduced to the status of subordinates to the new Secretary of State for Defence. This was achieved over the intense opposition of the services and was the result of the support given by the Prime Minister to Lord Mountbatten who, as Chief of the Defence Staff (1959–65), was a fervent exponent of defence reorganization and centralization. Thus, although the three services have retained their separate identities, their influence has been submerged in a single Ministry of Defence. Their only channel of communication to the Secretary of State is through the Chief of the Defence Staff who, as the Chairman of the Chiefs, no longer represents one of the services.

Since the First World War, with the growing technological complexity of modern warfare, the armed services have relied increasingly on the professional advice of scientists, engineers, chemists and technical experts of all kinds in the procurement of new weapons systems, planning and analysis. The defence establishment has become a complicated structure, with a plethora of interlocking committees, planning and steering groups, attended by civil servants, service personnel and experts of all kinds. In addition, each service has retained its own Board, responsible to the Defence Council, presided over by the Secretary of State, and which is concerned with matters pertaining to its own service: morale, recruitment, promotion etc. There is also a Central Defence Scientific Staff, supervised by the Chief Scientific Adviser, a Defence Operational Analysis Establishment and a Procurement Executive, to name but a few. The Procurement Executive was set up in 1972, under a civilian Chief Executive. Its task is to prevent the excessive duplication, cost overruns and long delays in the procurement of new equipment which characterized the 1950s and 1960s. It works closely with contractors to ensure that research into new projects is properly conducted and that the prices charged are reasonable. The Executive has not always been successful in checking overcharging by contractors, especially in spare parts, where a cartel appears to operate, but the situation is certainly an improvement on the previous system.

This somewhat cumbersome administrative structure makes it difficult for an outsider to detect where policy-making is located in the Department. It is often the result of successive inputs of recommendations and ideas at each stage of the planning process. The Secretary of Defence, particularly if a knowledgeable and able politician like Denis Healey, who held the office from 1964 to 1970, will define broad policy, in consultation with the Prime Minister and other senior colleagues in the Cabinet. The details are then worked out in the Department. At each level of the administrative process drafts and recommendations will be changed or overturned, both at committee stage and in consultation with under-secretaries and the Permanent Under-secretary. There frequently has to be close consultation with the Foreign and Commonwealth Office and other Departments of State, whose interests may be affected, involving a well-structured inter-departmental committee system.

Defence Secretaries may also go outside their Department for information and advice. Some have even used unofficial advisers, not connected with either the Department or the armed services. Leslie Hore-Belisha, Secretary of State for War in the late 1930s, relied for a time on the advice of a military expert, Sir Basil Liddell Hart, who advised the Secretary not only on strategic questions but also on promotions at higher command level. Naturally, this did not make either the Minister or Liddell Hart very popular with the officer corps. Duncan Sandys, who kept his plans secret from the service heads until he could present them with a *fait accompli*, appointed a former officer, Colonel Post, an acquaintance of his, as assistant in his private office.

In the 1950s a new breed of defence intellectual arose in the universities and in defence research institutions, independent of the services or the Ministry, like the Institute of Strategic Studies. Academics such as Michael Howard and Lawrence Martin and scientists such as Professors Zuckerman and Blackett became active in studying and writing about defence issues. Important contributions were made by journalists and defence correspondents such as Charles Douglas Home of *The Times*, Alistair Buchan and David Divine. Since then there has been a considerable expansion in the study of war and strategy in the universities and polytechnics, and a younger breed of defence analyst has emerged in this area. It is difficult, however, to assess the influence of these scholars on the formulation of policy. A former defence correspondent of *The Times*, Lord Chalfont, became Minister in charge of disarmament questions during the second Wilson administration, but this is rare, and the interchange between the academic world and the bureaucracy, which is accepted practice in the United States, is not so usual in the United Kingdom. While enlarging the area of public debate on defence and helping to dispel the ignorance and sloganizing that were characteristic of higher institutions of learning in the United Kingdom during the 1960s, their ideas usually have an impact on politicians who are already susceptible to them. Thus, the writings of Liddell Hart were well received by Neville Chamberlain and Hore-Belisha precisely because his advocacy of 'a British way in warfare' and 'limited liability' fitted in with their existing precepts about future British military policy.

Since 1957, successive British governments have been more successful than their predecessors in forcing policy changes through the defence establishment with its myriad vested interests. This has been assisted by the organizational changes and moves towards centralization which have taken place since the early 1960s and which have made it harder to frustrate new policies. The main impetus, of course, has come from politicians who have possessed the will and the political motivation to get their own way. The inexorable upward pressure of defence expenditure during the 1950s and beyond convinced the political leadership and the Treasury that drastic steps had to be taken if the estimates were not to spiral beyond control, while the financial crisis resulting from the Suez War provided the final push for the institution of reforms. Sandys's measures were dictated solely by financial considerations. The decision to abandon Britain's role east of Suez in 1968 was the culmination of a lengthy process of deliberation and debate, since hitherto both the Prime Minister and the Defence Secretary had been determined to uphold Britain's global role. Once again, severe economic crisis was the decisive factor which forced Ministers into the decision. It was then pushed through with complete disregard for domestic and overseas pressures, and in the full knowledge that the United States was anxious that Britain should remain east of Suez.

Another factor which played a major part in pushing the defence estimates upwards was the escalating costs of advanced technology which caused the price of both conventional and nuclear arms to rise to astronomical levels. The reductions in service manpower in 1957 and the further reductions during and after 1968 enabled the British Exchequer to meet these rising technological costs, although not without considerable strain. During the 1970s, despite the concentration of Britain's defence efforts on Western Europe, inflationary pressures ensured that there was no alleviation in the mounting costs of equipment, and politicians were forced to attempt palliatives, such as introducing managerial efficiency techniques into the Ministry of Defence, and to apply systems analysis methods to new weapons in the hope that these would lead to the requisite savings. At best the savings have been marginal, and in 1981 the government, in a new Defence Review, was compelled to propose further reductions in the service estimates, which chiefly affected the size of the navy. The Cabinet, however, was forced to abandon these plans by the Argentinian decision to invade the Falkland Islands the following year. With the shrinking in size of Britain's defence establishment since 1957, vested interests, such as defence contractors and others concerned with defence procurement, have also seen a diminution in their number and size, and as a result their influence, like that of the Chiefs of Staff, has been circumscribed.

That there have been striking changes in the size and

geographical location of Britain's armed services since the 1950s is obvious, as is the fact that the pressure to effect these reductions has not come from just one of the main political parties. Historically, given its anti-militaristic traditions, one would have expected the Labour Party to have taken the lead in calling for cuts in Britain's armaments, as it did with some success during its brief periods in office between the wars. The Attlee government presided over the reintroduction of conscription and the decision to construct the atomic bomb after the Second World War, and introduced an ambitious rearmament programme in 1950. During the 1930s, the Conservative governments insisted that there should be no massive rearmament in the face of the rise of the Axis powers. During the 1950s it was Churchill's government which reduced the size of the Attlee government's programme, and the Eden and Macmillan governments which sought large savings in the defence estimates, which Macmillan ultimately achieved. During the 1960s, the Wilson government clung tenaciously to Britain's role east of Suez despite mounting opposition from its own backbenchers.

Nor did extra-parliamentary agitation from the Campaign for Nuclear Disarmament have much impact on Labour government policies. Although it managed to sway Labour Party Conferences in its favour for a time in the 1950s and again in the 1980s, once in power Labour governments have generally ignored such pressures, keeping Polaris during the 1960s and updating it during the 1970s. Nor can it be said that the anti-nuclear pressures that captured the Party during Michael Foot's tenure as Labour leader did much to improve its electoral prospects – precisely the reverse in fact – while the Thatcher government purchased Trident from the United States despite much posturing on the part of the anti-nuclear groups.

Elements in the Conservative Party were vociferous in their protests about the Labour government's departure from east of Suez after 1968, and its leaders promised to restore some of Britain's responsibilities outside Europe while in opposition but, in practice, little changed when they eventually returned to power. The Heath and Thatcher governments made only perfunctory gestures in this direction, while the Thatcher government was forced by the crises in the Falklands and in the Persian Gulf to take action which it would otherwise not have contemplated.

There has always been an imbalance between the resources Britain has been prepared to devote to defence and the overseas commitments she has entered into. This remained true after 1945, although significant changes took place in the size and distribution of Britain's responsibilities during the succeeding decades. These changes seem to have taken place with little or no consideration of their diplomatic consequences. While Sandys at least attempted to justify reliance on the nuclear deterrent by referring to the importance this would have on restoring close relations with the United States after Suez, the decision to withdraw from east of Suez in 1968 irritated Washington and offended many of Britain's Commonwealth partners by the suddenness with which it was announced and undertaken. The Ministry of Defence's decision to withdraw Britain's ice patrol vessel HMS *Endurance* from Falklands waters in 1981 as part of the government's defence economies was greeted with dismay by the Foreign Office, which considered, rightly as it turned out, that this would be read by Buenos Aires as a sign that Britain was less than determined to defend her possessions in the Falklands. Nevertheless, the decision was not reversed until the sudden irruption of tension in South Georgia induced a sense of realism in the Cabinet and Ministry of Defence about the situation in the South Atlantic.

There has not, therefore, been close coordination between defence and foreign policies since 1945, as was illustrated during the Suez Crisis when the Foreign Office was seldom told what was going on. However, despite short-run discordances, in the long run the Foreign Office has adjusted fairly smoothly to the changes that have taken place in Britain's defence configuration, especially as successive Foreign Secretaries have shared in the decision-making process. There has been a certain long-run coherence in Britain's progression from a global power in 1945 to a regional power after 1970, while the adoption of a 'eurocentric' defence policy has made it easier for the Foreign Office to adapt its diplomacy accordingly.

The Falklands War was a signal success for both the armed services and the planning organs behind them. Like most of Britain's overseas expeditions, the task force was hurriedly assembled at the last minute and there was every possibility that it would share the fate of many of the others – that is, abysmal failure. The long and careful preparations for the invasion of Normandy in 1944 demonstrated how hazardous are the prospects for the success of amphibious operations and how much effort must be applied beforehand to ensure that sufficient resources are available at the right time and in the right place. The ultimate success of the Normandy landings was due to the success of the military planning organization behind it and the ability of the Supreme Commander, General Eisenhower, to inculcate a team spirit among a diverse group of officers from different backgrounds and nationalities.

Similarly, as Professor Freedman has recently pointed out, the success of the Falklands operation was assisted by the relatively harmonious and cooperative relations which prevailed among the War Cabinet, the Cabinet Office, the Ministry of Defence, the Foreign Office, the intelligence services and the overall commander.[1] Despite the inevitable tensions that arose, this situation compares favourably with the rivalries and jealousies which marred the conduct of the American intervention in Vietnam and subsequent military actions which that country engaged in. It was also a refreshing change from the mismanagement and divided counsels that characterized the preparations for the Suez expedition in 1956. Then the politicians attempted to harry the military into embarking on an expedition which the armed services were manifestly not ready to undertake at short notice, but which when eventually embarked upon came too late to prevent an outcry from international opinion. The Eden government's bewildering collection of public statements about the aims of the expedition caused confusion even among its own supporters. At the same time, public opinion and the political parties were bitterly divided about the merits of the entire enterprise.

By contrast, the Falklands War, from the assembly of the task force to the final denouement, was a short campaign, thus allowing little time for domestic opposition to develop while, unlike Suez, Britain had wide international support for her action. The issue was a straightforward one – the expulsion of an invader from British territory – and, despite arguments about some of the methods employed and about Britain's negotiating tactics, there was general agreement among Britain's political parties and the public at large on this.

The success of the operation was a welcome boost to the prestige of Britain's armed services and particularly to the army, after its thankless and bruising experiences in Northern Ireland. While there has been an appreciable decline since 1945 in the number of sons of traditional service families taking up commissions in the army, the Falklands experience demonstrated that the professional standards of the officer corps remain high and their quality has been maintained. Despite the often bewildering changes that have taken place over the years, the Falklands War has shown that the ordinary soldier, sailor and airman can give as good an account of himself in battle as his predecessor has done in the countless 'limited' wars in which Britain has been engaged since 1945.

Note

1 Lawrence Freedman, *Britain and the Falklands War* (Oxford, 1988).

2 Historical Background

In July 1945 the British General Election resulted in the defeat of Winston Churchill's wartime government and a huge majority for the Labour Party. Clement Attlee formed a Labour government which found itself grappling with awesome problems of post-war reconstruction and rehabilitation. Britain's economy had been severely strained by six years of war, her trade was in ruins and she had lost virtually all her pre-war overseas investments. Externally, she was faced with the task of governing and defending a sprawling Empire with resources which were barely adequate for the task. However, while her predicament was extremely serious, there was nothing new in this situation. During the nineteenth and twentieth centuries successive Chancellors of the Exchequer had complained about the excessive strains which were imposed on Britain's finances by the responsibilities of her overseas Empire, while the British army was at times almost overwhelmed by the difficulties of defending the internal and external security of Britain's widely dispersed colonies with inadequate manpower. 'We have not got the men to spare and that's the plain truth of it', the Secretary of State for India, John Morley, remarked when presented with a demand from the Indian government for the expansion of the Indian army in 1906.[1]

Britain's success in conquering and controlling her nineteenth-century Empire was based in large measure on a mixture of luck and bluff, and her military planning seemed more often than not to be based on the principle of 'muddling through', rather than on any careful assessment of means and ends. Of course, her international power and prestige were based on her possession of a large navy with bases across the globe, and not on her military prowess. She faced her most serious military challenge before 1914 during the Boer War in South Africa when in one week in December 1899 her armies were soundly defeated by the previously despised military forces of the Boer Republics. By denuding her garrisons in Britain and elsewhere of as many troops as possible, by appealing for volunteers and by using the manpower resources of her white dominions, Britain managed, after a long struggle, to defeat the Boers, but if a threat from the continent of Europe had arisen at the same time the War Office admitted that it would have been hard put to find enough troops to defend the United Kingdom from invasion.

At the end of the Boer War Britain began to reform her armed services. An Army General Staff was set up, with a Chief of the Imperial General Staff at its head, designed to coordinate planning and intelligence on an Empire-wide basis. When Richard Burdon Haldane became Secretary of State for War at the end of 1905 he embarked on far-reaching changes in the structure and organization of the British army, establishing an Expeditionary Force in Britain of 166,000 men by 1912 as a central reserve for use in the event of overseas (in fact, chiefly European) emergencies, and scrapping the various reserve and militia forces and replacing them by a Territorial Army which was to be a back-up force for the regular army. The First Sea Lord after 1905, Admiral Sir John Fisher, also reorganized the Royal Navy, scrapping large numbers of obsolete vessels, withdrawing naval forces from the Far East and the West Indies and procuring for the fleet in 1906 a new all big gun battleship, HMS *Dreadnought*, which was better armed and armoured than any battleship then afloat.

By 1906, the British government perceived in Germany a much more dangerous potential enemy than either France or Russia, who had been Britain's rivals in the nineteenth century. Germany possessed the strongest army on the Continent and after 1899 began to build a large navy which was regarded in Whitehall as a most serious potential threat to Britain's security both at home and overseas. She reacted by concentrating her fleet in the North Sea against Germany and by drawing closer to France and Russia. By 1914, her skilful diplomacy had led to the virtual isolation of Germany, whose only certain European ally was the ailing Austro-Hungarian Empire. Britain had been allied with Japan since 1902, had managed to remain on friendly relations with the United States and had entered into agreements with France and Russia which, while not committing Britain to war on their side, did lead to the three powers supporting each other diplomatically during numerous crises which occurred in Europe before 1914. Britain had also entered into military and naval conversations with France which, in the case of the British army, had resulted in arrangements being made for the despatch of the British Expeditionary Force to France in the event of Britain's involvement in a Franco-German war. It was this world-wide network of alignments and friendships that enabled Britain during the First World War to concentrate all her resources against Germany.

With the outbreak of war in Europe in the summer of 1914, Britain despatched to the Continent a well-equipped and well-trained army, although it was prepared only for a short victorious struggle upon which all Europe's generals based their strategies before 1914. Few politicians or soldiers had anticipated the long slogging match which was to ensue. The exigencies of the four years of bitter trench warfare on the Western Front after October 1914 eventually forced Britain to mobilize for total war and, in 1916, to conscript her young adult males for military service. By 1918, Britain deployed mass armies on the Western Front. By the time Germany signed an armistice with the Allies on 11 November 1918 the British Empire had lost 750,000 men.

As a result of her victories, Britain in 1919 had considerably expanded the size of her Empire, at the expense of the bulk of Germany's former colonies and by her control of the Middle East following her defeat of the Ottoman Empire. But the need to economize after such an exhausting war, and her continuing economic problems after 1919, meant that she found it difficult at times to defend her overseas possessions against internal dissent and, after 1933, from external threats. During the early

1920s the immense war machine which Britain had built up by 1918 was rapidly run down and further financial sacrifices were then imposed on the armed forces in an effort to cut government expenditure. The problems faced by the army and navy in attempting to maintain viable forces were compounded by the entry of a new aspirant for the limited defence funds available: the Royal Air Force (RAF), which had been set up as a result of the amalgamation of the former Royal Army Flying Corps and the Royal Naval Air Service on 1 April 1918.

Politicians discovered that the RAF could be used relatively cheaply to police parts of the British Empire, allowing for the withdrawal of army garrisons, and in 1923 it was promised extra funding to build up its metropolitan air force to 52 squadrons. The Royal Navy, which was still the Empire's first line of defence, was not seriously affected by the financial squeeze until after 1925, when the improved international atmosphere resulting from the signing of the Locarno Pact led to further falls in British expenditure on her armed services. The navy could not thereafter replace her ageing battleships.

The army suffered the most from these post-war economies. After 1919, soldiers returned to their traditional tasks of policing the Empire – 'real soldiering' in the eyes of many long-term regulars – and it seemed unlikely that Britain would have any cause to send her Expeditionary Force to the Continent in a situation where her major potential enemies, like Germany, were still suffering from their defeat in the recent war or, like Russia, were exhausted from years of war and civil war. In any case, neither public nor politicians wanted any repetition of the enormous loss of blood and treasure which Britain had suffered on the Western Front between 1914 and 1918.

This climate of austerity did not encourage experiments in the new techniques of warfare which Britain had pioneered during the First World War, particularly in the deployment of tanks, which many military enthusiasts saw as the means of achieving rapid victories in the future. Such experiments as there were in tank warfare were left to a few devoted tank officers like General J. F. C. Fuller, who later became a famous writer on military subjects, but who soon became disillusioned by the niggardly financial support for tank training from the

War Office and by the vociferous opposition of military conservatives in the army to his ideas.

By the early 1930s Britain was facing a renewed threat in Europe from Germany, where Adolf Hitler became Chancellor in 1933. Her relations with Japan in the Far East had begun to deteriorate after Japan invaded Manchuria and then began to encroach on China proper after 1931 (the Anglo-Japanese alliance had been abrogated in 1922). Then in 1935 Britain quarrelled with Italy over the latter's invasion of Ethiopia. By 1939, Britain faced a potential combination of enemies on three widely dispersed fronts, in a situation which boded less well for her ultimate success than in 1914. Then she had possessed a modern navy and a fairly efficient army, while she had been able to concentrate the bulk of her forces against Germany. None of this applied in the 1930s, when she feared that if she became involved in a war with one of her potential adversaries, the other two would take advantage of this situation by intervening against her elsewhere. The United States, who had entered the First World War on the side of the Allies in 1917, had withdrawn into isolation after 1919, and during the 1930s the United States Congress passed neutrality legislation designed to prevent Britain or other belligerents in a future war from securing American loans. American loans had sustained the British war effort between 1914 and 1918. Many Americans believed that the protection of these loans had prompted American intervention in 1917, and they were determined that there should be no similar pretext for American involvement in any future conflict. Britain's only certain ally was France, herself distracted by serious domestic difficulties after 1932, while the Soviet Union was widely distrusted in British Conservative circles.

After 1934 Britain tried to remedy the worst deficiencies in her armed services which had been accumulating since 1925. After the financial crisis of 1931, however, Britain was reluctant to strain her economy further by embarking on an all-out rearmament programme. Even if she had wished to do this, her inadequate military industrial base, which had suffered serious contraction as a result of the retrenchment after 1919, her shortages of skilled labour for both the civilian and military sectors and the need to ensure that raw material supplies for her export industries were sustained, made it impossible for her to expand her output of military equipment very much in the short run. Britain therefore concentrated on trying to build up a large bomber air force in a vain attempt to deter Germany, and in improving the quality of her navy as a means of countering any Japanese threat to her interests in the Far East. Inevitably, the army received only a tiny proportion of the extra defence expenditure which the Treasury grudgingly allocated to defence between 1934 and 1938, and by 1937 it still remained doubtful if Britain would send an Expeditionary Force to assist France in the event of war with Germany.

With Germany becoming even more of a threat to European peace in 1939, the British government at last launched a crash rearmament programme, introduced conscription and promised to send an Expeditionary Force to France. However, it was too late: with the outbreak of war in September 1939 Britain was inadequately prepared for a continental war. The defeat of France in June 1940 left Britain alone to face the Germans, but fortunately she had, after 1937, devoted more resources to fighter and anti-aircraft defence, and these and the use of radar to detect incoming hostile aircraft, enabled her to defeat Germany's aerial offensive in the late summer and autumn of 1940. But it was a close run thing, and it was only Hitler's invasion of the Soviet Union in June 1941, and his declaration of war on the United States after the Japanese attack on Pearl Harbor in December 1941, that enabled Britain both to survive and to emerge from the war in 1945 as one of the victor powers. But the effort had been an exhausting one and her survival had been dependent on American lend lease supplies and the despatch of American troops to Britain to participate in the invasion of Normandy in 1944. By 1945, it was clear that Britain had become the junior partner in the war effort.

Note

1 C. J. Lowe and M. L. Dockrill, *The Mirage of Power: British Foreign Policy 1902–1922* (3 vols, London, 1972), vol. 1, pp. 63–4.

3 From the End of the Second World War to the Korean War, 1945–1950

Public optimism in 1945 that the end of the long and gruelling war in Europe and Asia heralded an era of permanent peace was rudely shattered by the onset of the Cold War during and after 1947. The confrontation between the Soviet bloc and the West, now led by the United States, assumed many of the features of the 'armed camp' which characterized the relations between the European powers before 1914, although now with the crucial difference that the development of the atomic bomb made it increasingly impossible for the two blocs to contemplate all-out war, which would lead not to victory in any real sense, but to their mutual destruction. Thus, mutual distrust and antipathy dominated the relations between the two blocs, with the growth of rival alliance systems and frequent crises, any of which might have escalated into war – and, after 1950, a frenzied arms race.

These international developments seriously affected the British economy, already severely damaged by the ravages of the Second World War, since they suggested that Britain would have to maintain a relatively high level of defence preparedness, thereby adding to her already onerous burdens. Fortunately, before 1950 she was able to avoid any major additional contribution to West European defence since she was already heavily committed militarily to the Middle East and Far East, where a Communist uprising had broken out in Malaya in 1947, the first of many such insurrections in her colonial Empire.

The government took the decision in 1946 to develop a

British atomic bomb, which was likely to be another expensive undertaking in the absence of American assistance. The Attlee administration attempted to rationalize the defence establishment and to impose controls on defence expenditure, but it was an uphill task. Between 1945 and 1950 the British government attempted to cope with a myriad of defence problems at home and overseas in an economic situation which appeared before 1950 not to be improving, but rather to be steadily deteriorating.

Britain, the United States and the beginning of the Cold War, 1945-1947

With the ending of the Second World War there was considerable optimism in Britain about the future. The Labour government was committed to maintaining full employment and to a programme of domestic reforms in health, welfare and education. There was every expectation that the wartime coalition of Britain, the Soviet Union and the United States would continue. Much faith was put in the United Nations as a mechanism for preserving world peace. Britain's armed services were rapidly run down as servicemen and their families clamoured for demobilization. Conscription was abolished and defence estimates were drastically curtailed.

Of course, defence remained a serious and pressing problem. Senior Ministers in the new government were well aware of the disastrous consequences of Britain's weak military posture before 1939. Clement Attlee, the Prime Minister, had been an officer during the First World War and, as a former parliamentary under-secretary of war, regarded himself as a military reformer. The Chancellor of the Exchequer, Hugh Dalton, had campaigned vigorously during the later 1930s to instil into the Labour Party a greater sense of realism about the international situation at a time when the Party was dominated by anti-war sentiment and when Labour MPs voted regularly in the House of Commons against increased military estimates. The Foreign Secretary, Ernest Bevin, had been a trade union leader, and had considerable experience of the obstructionist tactics of Communists, and when he attended the Potsdam Conference in August 1949, he discovered that Soviet Communist leaders could be equally obstructive in international negotiations. Many of the Labour Ministers had served in Winston Churchill's wartime coalition government and, as a result, had some familiarity with the realities of power politics.

Nevertheless, the new government was in a difficult position if it sought to embark on a fundamental reorganization of British defences. Ministers concentrated on domestic and economic affairs and, as a result, defence did not have high priority on the new administration's agenda, except in so far as steadily increasing costs were having a devastating effect on Britain's already weakened economy. Yet reductions in expenditure, over and above the savings made as a result of the run down of the huge wartime service establishment, could not easily be contemplated in a situation where, as a result of her victory, Britain was in occupation of even more territory (reconquered from the Axis powers) than she had been responsible for in 1939. Admittedly, some of these additional burdens were temporary since they consisted of areas which had been part of the empires of France (Indo-China) and Holland (Indonesia) before the war which British forces would soon evacuate and restore to their former rulers. However, Britain would remain responsible for the security of India and Ceylon (until 1947 when they were granted their independence) and of Malaya and Hong Kong, for maintaining occupation forces in Libya, the British zone of Germany and north Italy (the last three being new and onerous burdens), large garrisons in Egypt and Palestine, with alliance commitments to other Middle East countries, troops in Greece assisting government forces against a Communist uprising and finally the few troops she kept in her African colonies. Political and financial pressures forced Britain to abandon Greece and Palestine in the late 1940s but this still left her with formidable burdens.

Her predicament became even more uncomfortable during and after 1946 when the wartime Anglo-American–Soviet alliance began to break down. The expectations of 1944 and 1945 that the big three great powers would continue to work together through the United Nations soon evaporated as relations between the Soviet Union, on the one hand, and the United Kingdom and the United States, on the other, became increasingly hostile. By 1947 the Soviet Union had sealed off Eastern and Central Europe (areas which she had overrun during the latter stages of the war) from all contact with the West. Germany, which had been divided into four zones in 1945 – American, French and British in Western Germany and Soviet in Eastern Germany – but which the allies had agreed they would operate as a single economic entity, was also becoming divided into two as the Soviets began to deal with their own zone in the east in isolation from the rest of the country. The Soviet Union was also behaving increasingly provocatively towards British interests in Greece and Iran, but Britain was in a difficult position economically and militarily to counter her on her own.

Churchill had long appreciated that both Britain's post-war security and her economic recovery depended on the continuation of the Anglo-American alliance into the peace, and Attlee was equally anxious that the close relationship which had been established with Washington after 1941 should not be impaired. It became clear in 1945, however, that Washington did not share this enthusiasm. The close wartime collaboration between the two countries was gradually brought to an end by Harry S. Truman, who became President of the United States in April 1945 on the death of Franklin Delano Roosevelt. Low-level military contacts were, however, allowed to continue. Britain's imperial role was subjected to much criticism in the United States, where many Congressmen suspected that British eagerness to keep on close terms with Washington was motivated by her keenness to secure American financial and military assistance to prop up the British Empire. In addition, many Republicans regarded Britain's Socialist experiment with ill-concealed repugnance.

Perhaps the most grievous blow for the British was the American decision to abandon the wartime cooperation between British, American and Canadian scientists on atomic research. Before 1941 British scientists, assisted by French scientists and other refugees from Nazi-occupied Europe, had made considerable progress towards developing an atomic bomb. However, once the United States became involved in the war it was agreed that the British scientists should continue their work in the United States in cooperation with their American counterparts; the United States had the resources necessary to pursue the research, while Britain remained vulnerable to Nazi aerial attack. Thus, British nuclear physicists emigrated to the United States to help complete the work of the so-called Manhattan Project, as quickly as possible and in advance of the Germans. During the latter part of the war President Roosevelt had signed two agreements with the British and Canadian governments: the Quebec Agreement of 19 August 1943 and the Hyde Park Agreement of October 1944. The Quebec Agreement bound the parties:

> first, that we will never use this agency against each other. Secondly, that we will never use it against third parties without each other's consent. Thirdly, that we will neither of us communicate any information about Tube Alloys [the British code-name for the project] to third parties except by mutual consent. Fourthly, that in view of the heavy burden of production falling upon the United States as a result of a wise division of the war effort the British Government recognise that any post war advantages of an industrial or commercial character shall be dealt with as between the United States and Great Britain on terms to be specified by the President of the United States to the Prime Minister of Great Britain.[1]

The final section was the product of American suspicions that the United Kingdom might subsequently reap the financial benefits of the huge sums of money the United States had invested in the project. The Hyde Park Agreement abandoned this clause and stated that: 'full collaboration ... for military and commercial purposes shall continue after the defeat of Japan unless and until terminated by joint agreement.'[2]

However, these agreements were executive ones signed by the President only and they were not approved by the United States Congress. Hence they were not binding on future administrations, as the British were to discover when Truman took over the presidency. After 1945 Britain's scientists encountered increasing obstruction from their American counterparts when they sought information about the progress of atomic research in the United States. It soon became clear that the United States was determined to retain her monopoly over the secret of the atomic bomb, although she claimed that her unwillingness to divulge information to the British resulted from her desire not to alienate the Soviet Union by presenting her with an Anglo-American bloc at a time when the United States was striving for some form of international control under the so-called Baruch Plan.

In an effort to find out what United States' plans were for the future and to try to ensure that the United States lived up to its wartime agreements, Attlee and Mackenzie King, the Canadian Prime Minister, visited Washington in November 1946. They discovered that Truman did not know of the existence of the Hyde Park Agreement, while he claimed that the Quebec Agreement did not, in his view, commit the United States to share information with the other two powers. However, on 16 November he was persuaded to sign a memorandum in which it was stated that 'we desire that there should be full and effective cooperation in the field of nuclear energy between the United States, the United Kingdom and Canada.'[3]

However, British scientists soon found that despite this agreement their American counterparts were as reluctant as they had been before to provide them with technical information. The Americans feared that the United Kingdom would use this to produce an atomic weapon of its own. Truman insisted that the November agreement did not bind the United States to divulge information of more than a general nature. Clearly, since Congress was taking a close interest in the question, Truman was more concerned about the domestic considerations involved than in future cooperation with the former allies of the United States. This was clearly a blatant attempt to preserve the American monopoly over the bomb.

On 1 August 1946 Congress passed the McMahon Act which prohibited any sharing of nuclear information with other powers, and thereafter the flow of information to British scientists ceased altogether. The Attlee government was faced with a serious dilemma. While Britain possessed considerable scientific expertise about the bomb, its production would require the provision of expensive manufacturing facilities which would severely strain Britain's already overburdened exchequer. On the other hand, if Britain was to retain her status as a great power, her possession of the atomic bomb was essential. Furthermore, in the absence of any sign of American concern about the defence of Western Europe, and given the weakness of the French and British armies in the face of possible Soviet aggression, a British bomb appeared to be the only means of resisting a Soviet threat to Western Europe. Accordingly, in 1946, a secret Cabinet Committee of senior Ministers, with Attlee in the chair, authorized the production of a British nuclear device: this decision was concealed from the rest of the Cabinet and Parliament until the early 1950s, while the expenditure was buried in miscellaneous estimates. In 1948 the Chiefs of Staff told Attlee that Britain needed at least 200 bombs if Britain's defence posture was to be a credible one.

Thus, until the United States was prepared to resume nuclear cooperation with the United Kingdom, the British government was determined that Britain would produce a bomb by her own efforts. There was, however, little sign that the United States would relax her rigid attitude towards the transfer of nuclear information. Indeed, in 1947 Congressional pressures forced Britain to abandon her right of veto over the use of the bomb, although a vague promise of consultation was substituted, while the arrest in February 1950 of Dr Klaus Fuchs, a scientist who had worked on the Manhattan Project during the war and at the British nuclear research establishment at Harwell after 1945, for passing atomic secrets to the Soviet Union convinced many American legislators that the United Kingdom could not be trusted.

The British decision to proceed with the development of an atomic bomb was an important demonstration that the Cabinet was determined that, despite her post-war economic difficulties, the United Kingdom was to remain a major world power. Britain had emerged as the only Western European power not to be overrun by the German army, and her solitary stand against Nazi Germany in 1940 and 1941 had been an inspiration to many, and not least to the British themselves. As well as emerging from the war as a major victor power, she controlled large areas of the world's surface and deployed substantial ground, air and naval forces on a global scale. Given the destruction that had been inflicted on Germany and Japan, her major pre-war trading competitors, there seemed no valid reason why she should not restore and even expand her export trade, which would in turn enable her to recover her economic strength. Her main difficulty in the immediate post-war years was that in order to reconvert her war-torn industries to civilian production she needed to earn sufficient dollars to enable her to purchase much-needed raw materials and manufacturing equipment from the United States, the only country whose economy had thrived during the war. To this end she negotiated a loan from the United States in December 1945, although as part of the deal she was forced to agree to dismantle her system of imperial tariff preferences and to promise to restore sterling to full convertibility with the dollar by 1947, both of which requirements involved her in further short-term financial difficulties. At the same time, her dependence on the United States for financial assistance made her reluctant to quarrel with Washington over the nuclear issue.

The basis of Ernest Bevin's foreign policy was the belief that the United States would soon overcome her reluctance to become too closely involved with Western Europe and would eventually decide that her own interests required her to come to the assistance of the area militarily and economically. He anticipated that, as a result, the so-called 'special relationship' between the United States and the United Kingdom would be restored, given that the United Kingdom was the strongest anti-Communist power on the Continent. In the event, Bevin's hopes were realized: the post-war drift in American foreign policy, which had given rise to fears in London that she might revert to the isolationism of the inter-war years, was soon replaced by an increasingly antagonistic attitude towards the Soviet Union, whom the United States accused of wrecking any chance of cooperation between the two powers by her hostile policy towards the West, and by her efforts to extend her 1945 acquisitions in Eastern and Central Europe into the Mediterranean and the Middle East.

Indeed, the increasingly bitter feelings towards the Soviet Union in the United States were expressed in the crudest anti-Communist terms, which Truman justified on the grounds that such emotive language was the only way of galvanizing cost-conscious American Senators into voting the sums necessary to enable the United States and her allies to resist the Soviet Union. As Bevin had anticipated, the United States took over Britain's financial burden in assisting the Greek government in the civil war in Greece, when Britain threatened to evacuate the country in April 1947. This was followed in 1948 by the passage through Congress of the Marshall Plan, which provided American dollar aid to help West European economic recovery, and which further widened the breach between the United States and the Soviet bloc.

Britain's imperial problems, 1945–1950

This welcome sign of growing American involvement in Western Europe did not, however, do much to help solve Western Europe's pressing military problems. Indeed, the Europeans felt helpless in the face of the large number of Red Army divisions based in Eastern Europe. Britain felt she could do nothing to help stem a Soviet invasion of the Continent, and planned to evacuate her occupation forces in Germany to the United Kingdom in that event. Imperial problems remained her major preoccupation. While the granting of independence to India and Ceylon in 1947 alleviated her financial problems to some extent, it increased her military problems since, with the refusal of India to cooperate with Britain in the defence of the region, Britain lost the valuable reserve of Indian troops she had previously drawn upon for service in the Middle and Far East, although Ceylon allowed Britain to use her naval base at Trincomalee.

The loss of the Indian Sub-Continent ought to have led to a far-reaching re-examination of Britain's future in the Middle East. Her preponderance in this vast area had been secured in order to defend the approaches to India. This justification was now no longer valid. Indeed, Attlee did suggest that Britain cut her losses in the Middle East by evacuating the Suez Canal and concentrating her defences in the future in the Western Mediterranean and the Atlantic Ocean, but in the face of the overwhelming hostility of the rest of the Cabinet and Chiefs of Staff to this proposal, he did not pursue the matter. Long-standing traditions were difficult to eradicate, and many of Attlee's colleagues firmly believed that Britain still had a crucial role to play in the Middle East. Indeed, instead of reducing her presence in the Middle East, Britain, over the next few years, spent large sums of money and considerable effort in trying to build up the area as a sphere of British power and influence.

There were, of course, tangible reasons why Britain decided to remain in the Middle East. Irrespective of the loss of India, she still depended on oil supplies from Iran and the Persian Gulf, which contained 30 per cent of her overseas investments in the 1950s. Britain had made strenuous efforts during the Second World War to defeat the German and Italian forces in North Africa and her control of the region was one of the few visible signs of her victory. Her troops were stationed in Egypt, Jordan, Iraq and Libya, although she withdrew from strife-torn Palestine in 1948. The Attlee government, true to its Socialist convictions, insisted that it would deal in the future with the Arab governments of the Middle East on terms of equality and would provide them with economic assistance in return for their agreement to new defence treaties with Britain to replace those signed in the 1930s. These were intended to be based on equality of treatment and on future Arab–British cooperation. Britain would also try to encourage the moderate nationalist forces in these countries instead of dealing exclusively as in the past with reactionary pashas and sheiks.

The Suez Canal base was intended to remain the heart of Britain's defences in the Middle East. Its central position dominating the Eastern Mediterranean and the Suez Canal (the route to the Red Sea and the Far East), the expensive facilities and military stores that the British army had built up there during the war and its proximity to North Africa and the Levant made it an ideal location for Britain's land, sea and air forces. The new Lincoln bomber had the range to attack targets in the Caucasus from Egypt, while Iraqi, Jordanian and Egyptian troops, with British logistical and air assistance, would hold the mountain passes of North Iraq in the event of a Soviet invasion.

The difficulty was that Egypt, the intended cornerstone of this edifice, was not prepared to cooperate with Britain by allowing British forces to remain in the Suez Canal. She refused to renegotiate the 1936 Anglo-Egyptian treaty which gave the British the right to garrison the Suez Canal base until 1956. Egypt insisted that Britain evacuate all her troops – about 75,000 men – from the base, although she was prepared to allow them to return in the event of a war in which Egypt was involved. This was totally unacceptable to the British who had no faith in Egyptian technical competence to maintain the base in a war-ready state so that it would be available for immediate British use in the event of hostilities. Furthermore, the complex planning and logistical problems which would be involved in arranging for the reoccupation of the base seemed insuperable. The British suggested numerous compromises, but since these all involved the retention of British military personnel in some guise in the base during peacetime the Egyptians rejected them. When, in 1951, Egypt denounced the treaty, Britain decided to remain in the base until 1956 in the hope that in the meantime the Egyptians would give way. However, as Egyptian nationalist fervour increased in the following years British forces in the base were subjected to sabotage and attacks by Egyptian guerrillas and, as a result, its utility as a centre for resistance against a Soviet invasion of the area became increasingly problematic.

With hindsight, it is clear that the rise of Arab nationalism after the Second World War was bound to make Britain's position in the Middle East untenable. In any case, the Arabs regarded the new state of Israel, established after the British withdrawal from Palestine and following a bitter war between Arabs and Jews, as a more immediate and dangerous enemy than the Soviet Union. Britain's efforts to deal even-handedly with the Arabs and the Jews in Palestine before 1947 had not endeared her to either side, while her standing in Arab eyes did not improve as a result of her reluctance to become involved on the side of Jordan and Egypt during the 1948 war. Furthermore, her weak economy made it difficult for her to provide the Arab states with much in the way of economic assistance, while the same consideration would prevent her from defending the Middle East without outside aid, although a 25-year defence treaty was signed with Libya in 1953.

With closer Anglo-American relations after 1947 Britain hoped that her task in the Middle East would be eased by American financial aid and even by American air, naval and ground assistance there. The American air force and navy were interested in the idea, but the American army was resolutely opposed to the employment of its forces in that theatre. Finally, in 1950, the United States Joint Chiefs of Staff told their British counterparts that they could expect no American assistance in the Middle East until at least two years after the outbreak of a global war. Britain eventually persuaded Australia, New Zealand and South Africa to promise to send some air and ground forces to the Middle East, but they would only agree to do this after hostilities had broken out and not before.

Britain was thus faced after 1945 with the same dilemma that had haunted her in the inter-war years: she possessed much overseas territory yet lacked the resources necessary to defend it effectively. This did not, however, alter in any way her determination to cling on to her status as a great power. The 1948 Defence White Paper insisted that while 'the security of the United Kingdom is one of the keystones of Commonwealth Defence ... equally the United Kingdom alone, without the support of the Commonwealth, would lose much of its effective influence and power.'[4] The theme of the importance of Britain's overseas role was repeated in the 1950 Defence White Paper, where it was stated that Britain's defence responsibilities were not restricted to NATO since 'the Middle East is a vital strategic area and the maintenance of our position in the Far East is essential to the security and well being of the Commonwealth.'[5]

As if to underline her insistence on maintaining her Far Eastern role, the outbreak of a Communist insurrection in Malaya, a vital source of rubber and other raw materials, in

1947, while it added to her burdens, was met by the prompt despatch of troop reinforcements to that country. As a result, Britain was involved in long drawn out operations in Malaya which did not result in the final defeat of the Communists until 1958. This was the first of many such guerrilla outbreaks in her colonies that were to preoccupy the army in the future. By 1951, Britain had 35,000 troops in Malaya fighting 8,000 guerrillas.

Britain, the United States and NATO, 1947–1949

In Europe, Britain and the West European states were too weak to resist a Red Army invasion, and both Britain and the United States planned to remove their occupation forces in Western Germany to Britain and the Mediterranean in that event. Such Anglo-American plans as there were provided for the defence of the British Isles and the Mediterranean until the British and Americans could build up their forces for a new D-Day invasion of Europe: it was not a very convincing scenario, although both the Royal Air Force and the United States Air Force claimed that their planes would shorten the war by pounding the Soviet Union from bases in Britain and Egypt.

However, the increasingly bitter Cold War atmosphere between East and West resulting from the Soviet blockade of the three Western held sectors of Berlin in the summer of 1948 prompted both the United States and Britain to reconsider the question of the defence of Western Europe. In 1947 the United Kingdom had signed a defensive treaty with France, the Treaty of Dunkirk, although this was directed against a resurgent Germany rather than the Soviet Union. Britain refused to extend this treaty to the other West European states in view of her inability to defend them. However, in order to encourage the growing American interest in Western Europe and to show her that the Europeans were willing to take steps to organize their own defence, she entered into a mutual security pact in the following year with France, Belgium, The Netherlands and Luxembourg (the Brussels Pact). This was directed against

Soviet aggression, but without the assurance of American backing Bevin realized that it had little credibility as a deterrent.

After much internal debate, the United States finally agreed to throw in her lot with the Europeans, and on 4 April 1949 she entered the North Atlantic Treaty Organization with the Brussels Treaty signatories, Iceland, Italy and Canada. This did not of course override the war-making power of the United States Congress; the United States promised only to treat an attack or threat to any member or members of the alliance as an attack upon or threat to herself, leaving it to Congress to make the final decision. As far as the Senate was concerned, in approving the passage of the necessary legislation for American membership of the pact, NATO was based on the principle of mutual aid. United States' financial assistance, provided for in an accompanying military assistance bill, was designed to help the Europeans to build up their own defences so that eventually they would not need to rely on the United States. Certainly, Congress did not envisage that any more American troops, in addition to the occupation forces already in Germany, would be sent to Europe.

Bevin welcomed the formation of NATO, which was very much the result of his exertions, since the United States was now firmly committed to West European defence. The Berlin crisis of 1948–9, when the Soviet Union closed the road and rail access routes to the Western sectors of Berlin for 15 months and an Anglo-American airlift kept West Berlin supplied with foodstuffs and other necessities, helped to persuade Congress to approve the NATO treaty and led to the stationing of American long-range bombers on British soil. Later, these would be nuclear capable, and could be used to bomb Soviet towns and industries in cooperation with the RAF while, after 1949, NATO forces would try to hold the line of the River Rhine against the Red Army. As a result of this decision, Britain was forced to reorientate her defence priorities towards Europe rather than concentrate her efforts in the Middle East.

Nor was there any alleviation of her financial difficulties until 1950. In 1947 she was forced to suspend the convertibility of sterling as a result of a serious drain on her meagre reserves, while in 1949 a further financial crisis led her to devalue the pound. Her occupation zone in West Germany was a further strain on her resources as she had to divert scarce foodstuffs, fuel and raw materials from her own economy in order to keep the Germans alive after 1945. She agreed to the merging of her zone with that of the United States in January 1948 in the hope that this would reduce some of her burdens there at American expense. Despite her lingering suspicions of the Germans, she came to accept the American thesis that Europe's economy would not fully recover from the effects of the war until West Germany, with her crucial Ruhr industrial complex, had fully recovered economically. This decision led to serious difficulties with the French, who refused to believe in the possibility of Germany settling down as a peaceful member of the European community.

British defence organization, 1945–1950

After 1945 British defence policy proceeded in a more or less pragmatic fashion, reacting to outside events rather than attempting to shape them, but Britain really had no alternative. The government did, of course, attempt to impose restraints on defence budgets. In 1946 the armed forces were informed by the Cabinet Defence Committee that they should base their future defence estimates on the assumption that Britain would not become involved in a major war for five years, and that even after that period had elapsed this would probably be extended to 1957. This was a pale reflection of the infamous ten-year rule which had been laid down by the Cabinet in 1919, whereby the armed services were to base their planning on the assumption that Britain would not be involved in a major war requiring the despatch of an Expeditionary Force to the Continent for ten years. In fact, the 1919 rule made little practical difference to Britain's armed services since economies imposed on them after 1920 had much more effect on their expenditures. Nor did it have serious implications for Britain's defence planning and on her defence industries until 1928, when it was extended on a yearly basis until 1932. Moreover, the belief that the United Kingdom faced no serious dangers for a number of years was as justified in 1945 as it had been in 1919. In 1919, Britain had vanquished her major enemy, Germany, while the Soviet Republic was involved in a bitter civil war: it would take the latter a long time to recover from the effects of this as well as from the destruction which had been inflicted on her before 1918. Similarly, although the Soviet Union was a victor power in 1945, it was reasonable for the West to assume that the immense loss of life and the terrible physical damage she had sustained during the Second World War would make it impossible for her to contemplate involvement in a major war for at least five years. However, the restrictions the British government placed on the defence budgets were dictated by economic factors and not by assumptions about the nature of the Soviet threat.

In any case, the five-year rule of 1945 was soon overtaken by the continued deterioration in the international climate, although even during the early 1950s defence planners clung to 1957 as the most likely date when the Soviet Union would be fully prepared for war. This assumption, however, was recognized to be a dangerous one since war could arise by accident or by miscalculation by one side or the other. Thus, while British defence expenditure did not rise sharply until 1951, continuing economic pressures in the late 1940s led the government to impose an annual ceiling on defence expenditure of £600 million in 1947 (this was increased to £780 million in the financial year 1950–1). However, the armed services still possessed ample stocks of arms, ammunition and equipment of all kinds left over from the Second World War and as a result they were unlikely to suffer from shortages of the basic weapons which were needed for the frequent counter-guerrilla wars in the colonies in which they were involved after 1947. Naval expenditure was also reduced. No more battleships or heavy cruisers were to be constructed, and those which had survived the war were to be phased out and scrapped. Since the Royal Navy's experiences with capital ships when they had been subjected to aerial attack during the war had been disastrous, their loss was not greatly mourned: the aircraft carrier was now regarded as a more versatile replacement, to a large extent self-defending and able to project its strength over long ranges.

The defence cuts after 1945 did, however, seriously impede the research and development of new weapons and weapon systems. Missile, jet bomber and fighter technology was particularly affected, while nuclear research absorbed much scientific expertise which might otherwise have been employed elsewhere. In 1947 specifications were ordered for a new generation of long-range jet bombers: the Valiant, Vulcan and Victor bombers which would not enter production until the mid-1950s. Until these more advanced types were available for service the Air Ministry ordered the crash production of the Canberra fighter bomber with a speed of 450 m.p.h. and a 2,100 mile range. These entered service in 1952 and were later armed with tactical nuclear weapons and transferred to the Second Tactical Air Force (TAF) in West Germany. Some 650 were procured and they were still being deployed in the 1970s.

The armed services were faced with acute manpower shortages in these years, with the army suffering the most, although the highly skilled men required in the RAF and the navy were also difficult to recruit. As industry and the economy recovered from the effects of the war, the demand for labour in the civilian trades increased and the armed services could not compete in this rising labour market especially as wages rose rapidly. In 1946 the government was forced to re-introduce conscription in order to ensure that the army in particular was provided with the necessary effectives. The period of conscription was for 12 months in 1946, but this was raised to 18 months in 1947, after the services complained that they could not train the recruits adequately in a year. When the Korean War began in 1950 it was increased to two years.

Conscription was a relatively inexpensive method of raising the forces necessary to cope with Britain's heavy overseas responsibilities but it was neither popular in the country nor was it an efficient means of running the army, while the other services complained that the skills necessary for their highly technical arms could not be taught and utilized properly even in 18 months. Nevertheless, although the total size of the manpower in the services was 1,512 million men in 1948, the largest peacetime forces ever raised in the United Kingdom after demobilization (although it fell to just over a million men in 1949), the Chiefs of Staff continued to complain that they were unable to discharge satisfactorily all the commitments that were imposed on them.

The government also believed that the way to both greater efficiency and economy in the defence establishment lay in the reform of its complex organizational and administrative structure. During the inter-war period such defence coordination as had existed was achieved through the cumbrous Committee of Imperial Defence (CID) and its multiple committee system. The CID, which had been set up by Prime Minister Arthur Balfour in 1902 in the aftermath of the Boer War and which consisted of senior Cabinet Ministers concerned with defence (the Secretaries of State for War and Air, the First Lord of the Admiralty, the Chancellor of the Exchequer, the Foreign Secretary, the Dominions and Colonial Secretaries etc. and their permanent under-secretaries and the Chiefs of Staff) normally chaired by the Prime Minister, was supposed to impose some order on service planning and to ensure that foreign, colonial and military policies were all working to the same end. It had never worked satisfactorily and was often the scene of angry clashes between vested service interests over their roles and missions. In 1923 a Chiefs of Staff Committee had been set up which was intended to present an agreed service view on strategy to the CID. More often than not CoS discussions resulted in a series of uneasy compromises between the different aims of the three services, while in effect each continued to go its separate way.

When, in 1940, Churchill became Prime Minister, he also conferred on himself the title of Minister of Defence which enabled him to take a close interest in all military matters connected with the war. Working through a small War Cabinet, he hoped to avoid the bitter in-fighting between the politicians and the leaders of the armed services which had characterized civil–military relations during the First World War. Attlee, who had taken an interest in military reform during the 1930s, had been impressed by the degree of coordination Churchill had achieved during the war, although of course his continual interferences in strategic and tactical questions had often exasperated the service chiefs. In 1945 the CID system was not revived. In December, Attlee appointed a committee composed of General Lord Ismay, Churchill's wartime Chief of Staff and Secretary of the War Cabinet, General Sir Ian Jacob and Lord Bridges, the current Secretary of the Cabinet, to make recommendations about the future organization of the British defence establishment.

The ensuing report, which was completed in February 1946, was a cautious document. It recommended the setting up of a Ministry of Defence which should be 'a guiding hand to formulate a unified defence policy for all three services'.[6] In fact, the functions of the new Minister were limited to trying to persuade the services to limit their expenditures and curtail some of their more extravagant plans. Such powers as he did possess derived from his membership of the Cabinet: the three service ministers no longer attended that body as of right. The Committee of Imperial Defence was replaced by the Defence Committee of the Cabinet, consisting of key Cabinet Ministers with the Chiefs of Staff in attendance, presided over by the Prime Minister, with the Defence Minister as vice-chairman. A Defence Research Policy Committee and a Ministerial Production Committee were also to be set up. The Attlee government accepted these recommendations, which were enacted under the Ministry of Defence Act of 1 January 1947.[7]

This reorganization was not a success. Attlee had overlooked the fact that Churchill as wartime Minister of Defence had been fascinated by all things military, had kept a close eye on all major strategic issues and, furthermore, possessed the powers to ensure that his orders were carried out. The post-war Ministers of Defence never possessed these advantages unless, like Duncan Sandys in the late 1950s, they had an iron will and the confidence of the Prime Minister. This was seldom true before 1957. The first Minister of Defence in the Attlee Government was A. V. Alexander (1949–50), previously First Lord of the Admiralty, but not a man possessed of a determined will. His successor, Emmanuel Shinwell (1950–1) had a livelier personality but tended to side with the Chiefs of Staff against the Treasury. For the most part the post was regarded as a political graveyard from which more able men escaped as soon as possible and, during the 1950s, few Ministers remained in the post for very long before they were promoted to higher office or disappeared into political oblivion. During this period the separate services pursued their own interests with little interference from the politicians, the only control over their powers came from the Treasury whose expertise lay in budgetary rather than in military matters.

Conclusion

In 1947 Britain granted independence to India, Pakistan and Ceylon, abandoned her Palestine mandate and handed over financial responsibility for her military effort in Greece to the United States. However, these extensive sacrifices did not presage the wholesale abandonment of the remainder of her imperial legacy. She did not consider that her other overseas possessions would be ready for independence in the foreseeable future. The Middle East now became the main area on which Britain was to concentrate her diplomatic and military efforts, seeking to maintain her hegemony there in cooperation with the Arab states in the region. When a Communist uprising occurred in Malaya Britain sent reinforcements to crush an insurgency which threatened her supplies of rubber and other raw materials, and as a result Britain became involved in a long drawn out campaign in the Far East.

After 1945, Britain was also faced with new responsibilities in providing occupation forces in Western Germany, Austria, North Italy and Libya. Despite her acute economic difficulties and the withdrawal of the economic, military and diplomatic support which the United States had extended to her during the Second World War, Britain had no alternative but to continue to shoulder these occupation tasks. Indeed, when the United States demobilized her wartime forces after 1945, Britain possessed the largest army in the West.

After 1948, however, with the onset of the Cold War, Britain could rely on renewed United States military and financial support to help her restore her shattered economy and underpin her overseas role. Nevertheless, her defence effort after 1945 involved her in heavy domestic sacrifices, including a wide range of controls over expenditure and investment and in the continuation of the rationing of food and clothing until 1952. In 1950, when the economy at last began to recover from its postwar difficulties, the Korean War plunged Britain into renewed financial difficulties. The underlying structure of the economy remained fragile.

Notes

1 A. J. R. Groom, *British Thinking about Nuclear Weapons* (London, 1974), p. 10.
2 Ibid., p. 13.
3 Ibid., p. 25.
4 Quoted in Sir Richard Powell, 'The evolution of British defence policy', in G. Frank, M. Imber and J. Simpson (eds) *Perspectives upon British Defence Policy 1945–70* (Proceedings of a Ministry of Defence Conference held at Winchester in April 1975), p. 49.
5 Ibid.
6 Franklyn A. Johnson, *Defence by Committee: the British Ministry of Defence 1944–74* (London, 1980), p. 19.
7 Ibid., p. 20.

4 From the Korean War to the Suez Crisis, 1950–1956

The Korean War compounded Britain's economic difficulties. Not only did she have to send substantial naval forces to Korean waters and a rather more modest army contribution to the United Nations effort, but the increased East–West tensions generated by the war forced her to embark on a major rearmament programme and to send major reinforcements to Western Europe. As a result, her finances were strained to the limit, and the onset of a new economic crisis after 1951 forced her to cut back the rearmament programme and to contemplate sweeping reductions in the size of her conventional forces. Her continuing heavy overseas commitments, together with bureaucratic and military obstructionism and administrative inertia, prevented any major reappraisal of defence strategy before the Anglo-French invasion of Egypt in 1956.

Britain's politicians and service chiefs had to cope with a seemingly endless series of international and imperial crises after 1950, and the concept of nuclear deterrence gradually came to be regarded by many in Britain's defence establishment as a relatively cheap yet potent solution to her military and financial difficulties.

The Korean War and British rearmament, 1950–1953

In Europe, Britain's commitments had expanded as a result of her membership of the North Atlantic Treaty Organization, although she refused to give her NATO partners any assurances that she would maintain her troops in West Germany indefinitely, especially as the establishment of the Federal Republic of Germany in 1949 out of the three Western zones of Germany suggested that West Germany would soon recover her full sovereignty. However, the North Korean invasion of South Korea on 25 June 1950 had far-reaching consequences for Western strategy, especially in Western Europe. The North Korean aggression coming so soon after the Soviet test explosion of an atomic bomb in August 1949, several years before many United States scientists thought this would be possible, and the Communist takeover of China in the autumn of the same year, convinced the Truman Administration that Communism was on the march in the Far East and that if South Korea fell, so would soon follow Japan, the Philippines and other areas in Asia vital to American security. Policymakers in Western Europe as well as in the United States believed that the North Koreans had been encouraged to take the action they did by the Kremlin, in the hope that a conflict in Asia would distract United States' attention and forces from Europe, thereby enabling the Soviet Union to blackmail the West Europeans into agreeing to a reunited Germany under Communist control.

The Truman Administration despatched air and naval assistance to the beleaguered South Koreans, and in July ordered American troops in from Japan. The United States also sponsored United Nations Security Council resolutions condemning North Korea for committing aggression and calling on United Nations members to send assistance to the South Koreans (the Soviet delegate had boycotted the Security Council in January as a gesture of protest at the refusal of the United Nations to seat Communist China). The United Kingdom and other Western powers reluctantly despatched token forces to South Korea as a sign of their solidarity with the United States. Although Britain did provide substantial air and naval support to the United Nations forces, her military contribution was a relatively tiny one. Later in the war a Commonwealth Division of British, Australian and New Zealand troops was formed to fight as a unit.

After April 1951 the war became one of attrition with savage offensives and counter-offensives across the 38th parallel, with the front moving little more than a mile or two in either direction. The British army gave a good account of itself: the action which attracted most press attention was the valiant stand of the Gloucestershire Regiment in April 1951 against a Chinese Corps which surrounded it. The Gloucestershires held on for a month before breaking out: only 39 men survived the ordeal.

As the war dragged on, Anglo-American differences emerged, especially after Communist China sent troops to assist the North Koreans in October 1950. Thereafter, the British government sought to encourage the Truman Administration to keep the war limited to the Korean peninsula in the face of strong domestic and military pressures to bomb Chinese Manchuria, with the consequent risk that the war would expand into a global conflict. The most serious incident, although much exaggerated at the time, was an alleged threat by Truman to authorize the use of the atomic bomb against China in November 1950: this sent Attlee scurrying across the Atlantic to secure assurances from the President that he would not use the bomb without first consulting the United Kingdom.[1]

The United States began to rearm in 1950. Truman had already ordered the development of the immensely powerful hydrogen bomb: the British government followed suit in 1952. The Korean War led the United States to expand the size of its conventional forces as well as its nuclear arsenal. The Attlee government, as a result of American pressure and the promise of further American aid, and anxious to prove its credentials as a close ally of the United States, also approved a large rearmament programme, requiring the expenditure of £3,700 million over three years from 1950, a sum which was increased to £4,700 million in January 1951. The Chancellor of the Exchequer, Hugh Gaitskell, a strong supporter of close links with the United States, believed that the British economy and balance of payments had recovered sufficiently to bear this increased defence expenditure, although Aneurin Bevan, the Minister of Labour, and two Junior Ministers resigned from the government in March in protest at the effects this level of spending would have on the economy and particularly on the social services.

In the end the Bevanites turned out to be correct in their assumptions. By the end of 1951 the economy showed signs of over-heating as defence contractors competed with the manufacturers of civilian goods for skilled labour, machine tools and raw materials. Raw material prices rose rapidly during the Korean War and this had a serious effect on Britain's balance of payments. The metal-producing industries were under increasing strain as orders poured in for iron and steel for the new tanks, guns, aircraft and other military equipment the Ministry of Defence was ordering. Furthermore, the promised American financial assistance never reached the figure that had been originally proposed. Inflation and balance of payments deficits soon began to mount. Even before the Attlee government fell from power after the October 1951 General Election, it had been forced to try to control defence expenditure by spreading it over a longer period than the original three years: the succeeding Churchill government began to reduce it altogether.

Thus the Korean War had a retardative effect on the British economy. It was to lead to a revival of Japanese industry, while West Germany was already recovering economically from the effects of the Second World War as a result of Marshall aid. Britain was to find these two countries formidable competitors in international markets as the 1950s progressed, while her own position was not made any easier by frequent labour disputes and the inefficiency of much of her management. Britain complained that her difficulties were compounded by the fact that neither West Germany nor Japan spent anything on defence in this period.

Nor was her rearmament programme very successful. The short period of expansion, followed by the imposition of new cuts, was not conducive to a coherent ordering of priorities. More money was invested in missile and rocket research and development, with some technical assistance supplied by the United States, but many of the missiles which emerged from the drawing board at the end of the 1950s were already obsolescent. Valiant bomber production was also speeded up in order that the first models could enter squadron service by 1955: meanwhile, the United Kingdom purchased 70 B-29 bombers from the United States. Specifications for the Centurion tank were also adopted.

The Global Strategy Paper of 1952

The test explosion of a British atomic bomb at Monte Bello Island in October 1952, the government's decision to develop the hydrogen bomb and the acceleration of V-bomber production (the first Valiant bomber squadrons became operational in 1955) all had important effects on British thinking about her future strategy. This was, of course, influenced largely by her continuing economic and financial difficulties, since nuclear weapons were coming to be regarded as a cheaper and yet more effective solution to Britain's defence problems. The Chief of the Air Staff, Sir John Slessor, was the prime mover in this reappraisal of defence policy. The Royal Air Force was convinced that the immense devastation it had inflicted on Germany during the latter years of the Second World War had made a major contribution to victory. The use of the atomic bomb by the United States Air Force on Hiroshima and Nagasaki in August 1945, followed almost immediately by Japan's surrender, seemed to clinch the argument of the air power lobby that they were now in possession of an awesome war-winning weapon which would relegate the army and the navy to the task of escorting convoys, defending air bases and occupying territory 'liberated' by the atomic bomb. This belief also had the advantage of giving them greater leverage in the competition between the three services for scarce defence funds, while Truman, before 1950, had made the atomic bomb the cornerstone of his deterrence strategy.

Slessor and the Air Staff had refined their ideas about future strategy more clearly by 1952 when, prompted by the government, Slessor met his fellow Chiefs of Staff at a special conference at the Royal Naval College, Greenwich in July and, after acrimonious exchanges, persuaded them to adopt the RAF's proposals in a Global Strategy Paper which was designed to settle British defence policy for the next decade. The contents of this paper are still classified but enough information has become available from other sources to give an indication of its broad outlines, while Slessor revealed his ideas in his book published later, *Strategy for the West*.[2]

The Paper described Britain's 'three pillars of strategy' as the defence of the United Kingdom, the retention of the Suez base on the route to the Far East and Australia and the maintenance of Singapore and Hong Kong. The Persian Gulf was also important and would need to be defended in an emergency. The Paper suggested that these heavy responsibilities could be significantly reduced if in future more weight was given in defence planning to the deterrent effect on potential adversaries of atomic and hydrogen bombs. An enemy would shrink from provocative actions against Britain's world-wide interests if he were aware that Britain was both willing and able to inflict unacceptable levels of damage to his cities and industrial infrastructure. Of course, Britain believed that in the event that hostilities did break out, the United States would be on her side and the combined effects of an Anglo-American nuclear attack on the Soviet Union would be so devastating that the issue would not be in doubt. The paper recommended that Anglo-American long-range air forces should be constructed for this purpose.

The authors of the Paper clearly anticipated that a British decision to adopt a strategy of nuclear deterrence would increase her value in American eyes, so that Britain's role as the major partner of the United States could be sustained indefinitely. If, however, the United States decided later to withdraw from Europe or refused to help Britain defend her vital interests, Britain would have sufficient nuclear strength of her own both to deter an enemy and to inflict devastating blows without American assistance. Slessor visited Washington during the summer of 1952 to impress his views on the Truman Administration, which did not, however, receive them with any enthusiasm, suspecting that this might be a British ploy to evade the recently agreed increases in her conventional military strength which had been accepted by all the European North Atlantic Treaty powers at a NATO ministerial meeting in Lisbon. However, his ideas were adopted by the Eisenhower Administration a year later.

Slessor was convinced that a strategy of nuclear deterrence, if allied to the development of so-called 'tactical' nuclear weapons (kiloton weapons equivalent to 1,000 tons of TNT), which were being developed in the form of rockets and shells for the British Army of the Rhine (BAOR), would significantly reduce the costs of Britain's defence, especially in terms of manpower. There were, of course, a number of flaws in his argument. Apart from the moral considerations which were argued vehemently later in the decade by the Campaign for Nuclear Disarmament, a grass-roots movement of protest against Britain's burgeoning nuclear arsenal which was to have considerable influence on Labour Party rank-and-file thinking during the 1960s and beyond, there were more practical objections to the strategy from the army and navy. Both services feared that their roles would be threatened if nuclear deterrence became a major plank in British defence policy. The army pointed out that nuclear weapons offered no solution to the problems of fighting guerrilla insurgents in overseas territories (a point which Slessor became more concerned about later) which required a substantial commitment of manpower and effort over a protracted period. Furthermore, neither the army nor the navy would accept the assumption that the use of nuclear weapons would be decisive in war. The navy had no intention of being relegated to the subordinate role of commerce protection and coastal defence, since it had invested much money and material in building aircraft carriers, which might become redundant if the RAF's ideas were accepted. Both services therefore insisted on the inclusion of a section in the Global Strategy Paper which referred to a lengthy period of 'broken backed warfare' which would follow the initial nuclear exchanges in a global war, and which would involve all three services in hard conventional fighting before the enemy was finally overcome. Thus the roles of the army and navy, and their respective shares of the defence budget, were safeguarded by acceptance of this doctrine.

Britain, Europe and West German rearmament

The new British emphasis on nuclear deterrence contradicted recent changes in NATO strategy to which the British government had agreed. Britain and her allies had accepted in 1950 that the left bank of the Rhine should be the West's main line of defence in future in the event of a Soviet invasion of Western Europe. However, this decision, while an improvement on her original plan to abandon the Continent altogether in the event of a Soviet assault, entailed the loss to the advancing Red Army of the bulk of West Germany, with its valuable industries. Moreover, the prospect that her territory would be occupied by the Russians was unlikely to appeal to the government of the Federal Republic of (West) Germany, which might, as a result of this strategy, decide to throw in its lot with the Soviet Union or declare its neutrality, when the West was anxious to attract the new state into its orbit.

Although both East and West continued to pay lip-service after 1950 to the idea of a future reunited Germany, it was clear before that date that this was unachievable on any conditions likely to be acceptable to one side or the other, and that the division of Germany into the Federal Republic and the Peoples' Republic of (East) Germany was to be a permanent one. Following the outbreak of the Korean War, the United States insisted that NATO agree to West Germany joining the organization so that West German manpower could be used for the purposes of West European defence. Britain and the United States had already contemplated this possibility before 1950, although Britain saw it as a gradual and long-term process, to be achieved only after the military strength, and hence the self-confidence, of the other European powers had revived.

The dramatic American demand for the immediate realization of this plan, which was put forward at a NATO meeting in New York in September 1950, came as a great shock to France, where continuing anti-German sentiment made it impossible for her government to accept voluntarily a German defence contribution to the West. France feared that this would lead to the reappearance in Europe of a German army, backed by considerable military industrial strength and with its own General Staff, which would in turn presage the renewal of the threat to Europe from German militarism. Given that the cream of the French army was fighting Communist guerrillas in Indo-China, French military strength in West Europe was totally inadequate to act as a counter to this threat. While the Americans accepted that some safeguards should be imposed on West Germany to prevent her becoming a danger to the rest of Europe, both Washington and Bonn insisted that West Germany's adherence to NATO should otherwise be on the basis of equality with the other allies. If NATO did not accept this demand the United States threatened to withdraw her offer to send four divisions of American troops to reinforce her occupation forces in West Germany, to appoint an American general (Dwight D. Eisenhower) to the post of Supreme Commander of Allied Forces in Europe and to provide any further military assistance to her allies.

In order to prevent the growth of an independent German army, and to persuade the Americans that France sought a positive solution to the problem of a German defence contribution, the French Foreign Minister, Robert Schuman, produced an alternative plan for the setting up of a European Defence Community (EDC) which would be based on the federal principle and would consist of a European army under a European Minister of Defence and which would have a common budget. In this organization, the armies of France and the other European NATO members, together with military formations provided by West Germany, would be closely integrated, thus effectively preventing the emergence of an independent German army with its own General Staff. The United States reluctantly accepted the Schuman Plan as an alternative to a long and contentious debate about its own scheme, which might have led to the collapse of NATO. Britain and the other European NATO powers, under considerable American pressure to do so, finally agreed in principle to the plan, although most doubted its military viability. Britain, however, refused to become a member of the EDC.

The Schuman Plan became the subject of lengthy negotiations after 1952. In that year NATO planners devised a more ambitious scheme for the defence of Western Europe than the existing one based on the defence of the Rhine. In future, NATO would engage in the 'forward defence' of Western Europe along the River Weser, which was close to the East German frontier near the Elbe. As well as protecting West Germany and its resources, this plan would give the West's defences a much greater depth than had been contemplated in 1950. The planners could now base their assumptions on a West German defence contribution in the future, but it was clear that if this new plan was to have any credibility the NATO powers would have to increase their military forces in Europe. Accordingly, at a NATO meeting in Lisbon in February 1952 the allies agreed to build up their forces in Western Europe to 50 divisions by the end of 1952 with a combined air force of 4,000 planes. Britain was to provide ten ground divisions. It was intended that the army divisions should rise to 96 by the end of 1960. Clearly, the implementation of this design would involve the European allies in great sacrifices, sacrifices which in the event they were unwilling to make.

This decision also contradicted Slessor's arguments that Britain should reduce her commitments on land by relying more on nuclear deterrence and ran up against the abhorrence with which many British politicians and service leaders regarded the prospect of a prolonged slogging match on West Germany's borders with the armies of the Soviet bloc. In May 1952 the EDC treaty was signed by the governments of the six continental European powers, but this was not the end of the matter: the treaty still had to be ratified by the parliaments of the respective signatories, and in the case of France this turned out to be a long drawn out process, as opposition to the EDC mounted in the Chamber of Deputies after 1952. Britain tried to encourage the French to ratify the treaty by entering into commitments to the EDC short of her joining the organization: this included a promise to increase her forces in West Europe to three or perhaps even four divisions and not to withdraw them except in the event of an emergency (in 1950 the United Kingdom and the United States had only two understrength divisions each in West Germany, when 14 NATO divisions faced an estimated 210 of the Eastern bloc).

Britain's continuing defence problems, 1953–1956

Despite much internal debate, British strategy during the early 1950s continued to be dogged by conflicting counsels, intense rivalry between the three services and expenditure beyond what the British economy could bear. In 1954, of a total number of army divisions of $11\frac{1}{3}$, $10\frac{1}{2}$ were stationed overseas: 4 in Germany, $2\frac{1}{2}$ in the Middle East, 2 in Malaya and the remainder in Trieste, Hong Kong and Kenya. Defence expenditure accounted for nearly 10 per cent of the total budget. Planning remained fragmented, while the advice of the Defence Research Policy Committee on future projects was usually ignored. Clearly, the 1947 reforms of the defence establishment had done nothing to ensure improved coordination or increased central control. Treasury control was also a broken reed: the Treasury's powers were restricted to bargaining with the individual service departments in the hope of persuading them to pare down their expenditure within an annual total agreed between Treasury and the Ministry of Defence, usually based on the previous year's estimates, and approved by the Cabinet. It was a laborious and time-consuming process in which the RAF and the navy were in a particularly advantageous position in that they possessed a strong lobby inside Parliament and in the armament industries which could always be relied on to exert strong pressure through press and Parliament when decisions crucial to their interests were about to be made.

Nor did overseas developments make Britain's search for a more rational and economical defence policy any easier. While East–West tensions relaxed slightly after the death of Stalin and the end of the Korean War, the Republican Administration of Eisenhower after 1953 viewed the Soviet Union as a dangerous adversary with whom genuine understandings were impossible. Nor did the rise of the mercurial Nikita Khrushchev to head the Kremlin hierarchy in 1955 do much to allay American suspicions of the Soviet Union, despite his repeated calls for 'peaceful coexistence' between the two blocs.

Khrushchev's blustering behaviour, his increasing tendency

to threaten the West with nuclear attack during crises and his reopening of the Berlin question during and after 1958 were hardly conducive to improved East–West relations. Nor was there much prospect of any agreement on arms limitation or even on a nuclear test ban in a period when the frenzied competition in nuclear and missile technology made it impossible for any of the great powers to risk falling behind their rivals. Moreover, the antagonism between the United States and Communist China did not diminish after the Korean armistice and on two occasions, in 1955 and 1957, Eisenhower threatened to use nuclear weapons against the mainland of China if Peking attempted to seize some offshore islands occupied by nationalist Chinese forces.

In this precarious situation, with Britain likely to be drawn into a Sino-American conflict, there seemed little Britain could do to reduce her escalating defence estimates except by minor cuts at the margins. Indeed, she saddled herself with even more overseas commitments during this period which made the armed services' opposition to any cuts easier to justify. In 1952 a rebellion broke out in Kenya against the colonial regime among the Mau Mau tribesmen, and this required the efforts of 3,500 British troops and local forces before it was finally put down in 1960.

The Middle East was becoming increasingly restive: in 1951 a nationalist Prime Minister in Iran, Mussadiq, expropriated the Anglo-Iranian oil company, a British concern, an action which threatened Britain's future as a major oil producer and supplier. For a time in 1951 Herbert Morrison, who had replaced the ailing Bevin as Foreign Secretary earlier in the year, contemplated the use of force to recover the company's sequestrated property and a naval task force was readied for that purpose. In the end, cooler counsels prevailed and the task force was used to evacuate British employees of the company from the main refinery at Abadan in September. A joint covert operation launched by the American Central Intelligence Agency and British Military Intelligence succeeded in August 1953 in destabilizing Mussadiq's government, allowing the Shah of Iran and the Iranian Army to recover their authority and overthrow the Prime Minister in the following year. Britain was forced to agree to the setting up of a new oil consortium in Iran in which United States oil interests received half the shares, although the Anglo-Iranian Oil Company was compensated for the loss of its interests in the country.

The Iranian oil crisis was a severe shock to the British government. It demonstrated the importance of secure supplies of Middle Eastern oil to Britain's economy and her balance of payments. It re-emphasized how important was the American connection to Britain in restraining the British from a violent response to the nationalization (Washington feared that this would lead to Soviet intervention), in trying to mediate between Iran and Britain and finally in cooperating with Britain to secure the downfall of Mussadiq without creating the appearance that this was the result of external pressures. The concessions that the American oil companies eventually secured in Iran angered many British politicians and businessmen and led to fears that Britain was slowly being edged out of the Middle East by the United States. The British were also concerned that the loss of prestige they sustained in Iran might encourage nationalists in other Arab states to seize British assets.

Britain's efforts after 1950 to persuade Egypt to allow British forces to remain in the Suez base proved unavailing and, faced with increasing Egyptian guerrilla attacks against her personnel and installations in the Suez Zone, and after Egypt had rejected a British offer to become a founder member of a new Middle Eastern Defence Command, the Foreign Secretary, Anthony Eden negotiated a treaty providing for the evacuation of the base by British forces by June 1956 with the military government of Egypt on 10 October 1954. However, British civilian technicians were to remain in Egypt to maintain the base for seven years, while in the event of an armed threat to Egypt, Turkey or any member of the Arab League, the base was to be reactivated, with British troops returning there. Clearly, however, in these circumstances, the Suez base would not be immediately available in the event of a crisis, but the British government hoped to overcome this problem by developing the island of Cyprus, which had been in her possession since 1878, as a military and air force base for 7,500 service personnel.

This led after 1955 to a confrontation with the Greek Cypriot community on the island, which demanded union (*enosis*) with Greece, an aspiration which clashed with Britain's determination to remain on the island. This new base also became a diminishing asset as Britain was forced to despatch troop reinforcements to deal with escalating Greek Cypriot terrorist outrages against her personnel and base installations.

Cyprus was intended to be the major British base in the Eastern Mediterranean from which she could attempt to sustain her dominance in the Middle East. In 1951, Britain promoted the formation of the Central Treaty Organization, or Baghdad Pact, in the region. This was created from a series of treaties between Britain, Turkey, Iraq, Iran and Pakistan directed against the Soviet Union. In the event of a Soviet invasion of eastern Turkey, CENTO forces would try to hold the Zagros Mountains on the Turkish–Iraq borders. The Soviets were estimated to have 24 divisions stationed in the Caucasus, while the CENTO powers between them could only muster about six.

The corollary was that only by deploying nuclear weapons could CENTO hope to defeat the Soviet Union. Here Britain's role would be crucial, since otherwise, as the Chiefs of Staff admitted in February 1955, 'we have neither the men nor the money to make the Baghdad Pact effective militarily.'[3] Britain's difficulties were made worse by the refusal of the United States to join the Pact, although she had encouraged its formation. Washington's view was that in terms of global defence Britain should be responsible for the Middle East, while the United States concentrated on the Far East. Only by deploying four squadrons of Canberra medium bombers in Cyprus, which British planners hoped would be possible after 1959, could there be any hope of the allies checking a Soviet advance by bombing her troop concentrations, ports and shipping from air bases in Iraq, while nuclear attacks on Soviet industries and command and control systems would, it was calculated, compel the Soviet Union to make peace. Britain's ground force contribution could therefore be restricted to logistical and other specialized troops and an armoured division. However, despite the emphasis on nuclear deterrence, Britain's commitment to

CENTO was still likely to involve her in considerable expense if the Pact was to evolve as a credible defence organization.

To make matters worse, Colonel Gamal Abdel Nasser, who had ousted the previous military government in Egypt and had appointed himself Prime Minister in 1954, denounced the Pact as a new method by which the Western imperialist powers sought to dominate the Middle East, by diverting the attention of the Arab states from the closer and more dangerous menace of Israel to the remote and implausible threat of the Soviet Union. In 1955, Nasser began to purchase arms from Czechoslovakia when the West refused to increase its arms supplies to Egypt, thus demonstrating to the Arabs that the Soviet bloc was not hostile to their interests but, on the contrary, was prepared to help with their defence. Furthermore, this meant that Egypt was no longer dependent on the West for its military hardware. Nasserite propaganda organs sought to turn Arab sentiment in Jordan and Iraq against their governments by appealing to Arab nationalists to unite against Western imperialism. As a result, the Jordanian government decided that its internal difficulties made it impossible for Jordan to join the Pact.

Britain was not only faced with this renewed threat to her position in the Middle East but she was also saddled in 1954 with another commitment, this time in the Far East. Encouraged by the United States, she agreed, on 6 September 1954, to accede to the South East Asia Treaty Organization, a loose alliance system comprising the United States, Britain, France, Australia, New Zealand, Thailand, the Philippines and Pakistan, directed against Communist aggression in the region. However, SEATO's constitution gave its signatories much more latitude than either NATO or CENTO in determining whether or not to intervene in a crisis and in any case Britain relied on American airpower as the mainstay of the defence of Western interests in the Far East, preferring to keep her ground forces there at a low level and for use in the defence of Singapore, Malaya and Hong Kong rather than being placed at the disposal of SEATO.

In Western Europe, the controversy over a West German defence contribution to West European defence threatened to impose fresh burdens on Britain. In July 1954 the French

National Assembly failed to ratify the EDC treaty and the entire question of a West German defence contribution had to be reopened. In an effort to settle the problem, Anthony Eden worked towards the direct entry of West Germany into NATO and the Brussels treaty. In order to encourage the French to accept this solution, Eden pledged that Britain would retain, for an indefinite period, four divisions and a tactical air force on the Continent. This reduced French fears that she might eventually be left alone on the Continent to face a resurgent Germany and, together with West Germany's voluntary acceptance of restrictions upon her rearmament, led to the settlement of this contentious issue in 1954. In 1955 Germany joined NATO and the Brussels Pact.

This was a historic decision. Apart from a brief period in 1939 Britain had never before accepted a peacetime commitment to come to the assistance of the Continent of Europe in the event of war. However, this sacrifice was more apparent that real. Britain assured her continental neighbours that she 'would maintain the present fighting capacity' of her forces in Europe, which enabled her to claim later that if her troops were provided with tactical nuclear weapons their 'fighting capacity' would have been maintained and even enhanced, which would permit her to reduce the number of her troops in the British Army of the Rhine.

Efforts to promote further defence cuts

In 1955, when Eden replaced Churchill as Prime Minister, he recognized that some more positive action would have to be taken to bring expenditure under control (see table 4.1). He wrote in his memoirs that 'the United Kingdom had attempted too much in too many spheres of defence, which had contributed to the economic crisis which every administration had suffered since 1945.'[4] R. A. Butler, the Chancellor of the Exchequer, warned the Cabinet that in 1955 the total defence budget would rise to £1,527 million and that, unless severe reductions were imposed, this would rise to £1,929 million by 1959–60. This was made even more pressing as a result of a

Table 4.1 Military manpower and defence expenditure in the 1930s and from 1947 to 1954

Year	Manpower (000s)	£ million	% of GDP
1932–7	326	153	3.1
1947	3033	930	8.4
1948	1512	740	6.7
1949	1066	770	6.5
1950	896	827	6.6
1951	890	1102	8.0
1952	932	1465	9.9
1953	958	1548	9.7
1954	957	1543	9.1

The proportions of the defence budget spent by each service during this period were roughly 35% for the army, 25% for the navy and 30% for the RAF.
Source: David Greenwood, 'Defence and national priorities since 1945', in J. Baylis (ed.) *British Defence Policy in a Changing World* (London, 1977), pp. 182, 186. Reproduced by kind permission of Dr Greenwood.

financial crisis in 1955, resulting from mounting inflation and a further deterioration in the balance of payments by £100 million.

Various attempts were made to ensure that the services concentrated in future on a more rigorous set of priorities. Selwyn Lloyd, the Minister of Defence in 1955, sought to stabilize expenditure at around £1,580 million for the rest of the decade. He wanted to abandon completely the assumption that a global war would be a long drawn out struggle, emphasizing that the nuclear deterrent would be decisive. More money would be spent on bombers and rockets, while the army and navy would suffer severe cuts. His proposals led to bitter recriminations from these two services, the War Office protesting that under them the size of the army would fall to 350,000 men, and the Admiralty claiming that the navy would lose up to two-thirds of its sea-going vessels, including minesweepers, submarines and coastal craft and carriers planned or under construction. The RAF also balked at the loss of coastal command and a reduction of the size of the Second Tactical Air Force. The Ministry of Defence proposed to reduce production of Valiant bombers and Hunter fighters and various missile projects such as tactical nuclear artillery. In 1956, the Corporal ground-to-ground tactical missile was purchased from the United States in an attempt to reduce the heavy costs of developing such weapons in the United Kingdom.

However, Selwyn Lloyd's suggestion that the services should also prepare to deal with Cold War crises overseas and meet Britain's 'political aims' left the services with considerable leeway to argue what should or should not be included under these categories. Faced with this concerted pressure, Selwyn Lloyd eventually abandoned his more ambitious schemes to achieve sweeping defence cuts and settled instead for more modest savings which would allow annual expenditure to fall to £1,640 million down to 1959, a figure which was well above the Treasury's predictions of what the economy could bear. In October 1955, Eden had considered reducing service manpower by 100,000 men. In December 1955, when Harold Macmillan replaced Butler as Chancellor of the Exchequer, and Selwyn Lloyd replaced Macmillan as Foreign Secretary, Sir Walter Monckton became Minister of Defence, a post he had not wanted and in which he was not interested. The search for financial savings languished during his period as Minister.

The Suez Crisis, 1956

The Suez Crisis of 1956 brought the debate to a temporary close. The situation in the Middle East had remained tense during the winter of 1955 and 1956. Nasser's anti-British propaganda campaign had reached new heights of virulence in early 1956. Eden now firmly believed that the Colonel was seeking to eject Britain entirely from the Middle East by undermining the governments of Arab countries friendly to British interests, like Jordan and Iraq, so that they were either forced to turn against Britain or were replaced by extreme nationalist elements who would certainly do so. Eden soon equated Nasser with Mussolini in that Britain was now faced with a dictator in the Middle East who sought Egyptian domination over the whole area.

However, Eden decided to make one further effort to bring Nasser into the Western sphere of influence by joining with the United States in financing the building of the High Dam at Aswan which would control the flood waters of the central Nile river and provide Egypt with hydro-electricity. Nasser regarded this dam as a significant contribution to the modernization of Egypt which he had set himself to achieve. However, the continuation of Nasser's anti-British campaign convinced Eden that the Egyptian dictator's ambitions were not to be stopped by concessions while Nasser's decision to recognize Communist China in July was regarded by John Foster Dulles, the American Secretary of State, as clear evidence that Egypt was drifting into the Communist bloc. On 19 July 1956, therefore, the two countries cancelled their loan offer.

Nasser retaliated by nationalizing the Suez Canal Company on 26 July, the bulk of whose stocks were held by the British government and by British and French financial interests and whose continued control of the Canal was regarded by London as essential if Britain's route to the Gulf and the Far East was to remain secure. Eden received the news with consternation, and that evening called a meeting of his senior Ministers – Lord Salisbury, the Secretary for Commonwealth Relations, Lord Kilmuir, the Lord Chancellor, Lord Home, the Secretary for Commonwealth Relations and Selwyn Lloyd – together with the three Chiefs of Staff, Sir William Dickson, Chief of the Air Staff, Lord Mountbatten, Chief of the Naval Staff and First Sea Lord and Field Marshal Sir Gerald Templer, the Chief of the Imperial General Staff, to discuss what steps Britain should take to recover the Canal. Eden recalled his experiences as Foreign Secretary in the 1930s, when the failure of the British government to take a firm line in resisting the Axis powers had encouraged them to continue their aggressive policies. He was determined that Nasser should be brought to a halt before he went any further in undermining the status quo in the Middle East.

This small group of Ministers and service chiefs constituted what became the Egypt Committee which, with the subsequent inclusion of the Minister of Defence, comprised the decision-making body for the policy which led to the Suez War. Apart from the members of this Committee, Whitehall as a whole was given hardly any information about its plans, and the need for close secrecy also resulted in the Cabinet receiving only the sketchiest information about what was going on.

On 27 July the Cabinet agreed that 'Her Majesty's Government should seek to secure, by the use of force if necessary, the reversal of the Egyptian Government's action to nationalize the Suez Canal Company.' Two days later the Egypt Committee decided that the best way of achieving this goal was to bring about the downfall of Nasser by a military *coup de main* in the hope that this would lead to his replacement by a more moderate government in Cairo which would negotiate a settlement of the Canal issue favourable to the West. The Chiefs of Staff were instructed to draw up an operational plan for an assault on the Canal, and France, equally angered by the loss of her investment in the Canal and by the aid and comfort Nasser was giving to the Algerian rebels, was to be approached to see if she would cooperate in the venture. France was to offer 35,000 troops (with a parachute brigade) and 200 planes as her contribution to the invasion force.

While three aircraft carriers were sent to the Mediterranean, air reinforcements despatched to Cyprus and 25,000 army reservists recalled to the colours on 2 August, Eden was considerably irritated to be told by the CoS that the United Kingdom could not mount a sudden assault on Egypt and that an invasion would take at least six weeks to organize. The three divisions of British troops which would be required to deal with Egypt's three infantry divisions and her armoured division (which included 100 modern Soviet tanks) would require a long period of thorough training, while armoured vehicles and tanks would have to be assembled and taken by sea to the landing areas. Moreover, given that Egypt had recently taken delivery of 100 advanced Soviet MIG and Illuyshin fighters, together with Soviet advisers to train the pilots, Britain would have to build up a large air force on Cyprus to neutralize the Egyptian air force and support the landings.

The French operation soon became exasperated by the frequent delays and changes of plan on the British side. The problems were endless. Cyprus was useless as a naval base and the task force would have to assemble and sail from Malta, the nearest deep water harbour. Since Alexandria was closer to Malta and Cyprus and within striking distance of Cairo, it was initially decided that the landings should take place there. Some 80,000 men would be landed on 15 September to secure the Canal by the eighth day. This plan, code-named 'Operation Musketeer', was further delayed by shortages of modern equipment for the landing force – only two tank landing craft and ten infantry landing vessels – and by the discovery that the few obsolete transport planes Britain possessed were not suitable for carrying the parachutists who were to spearhead the landings, without considerable modification. Some consideration was given to using Libya as the jumping off ground for the invasion but this was soon discarded as impracticable due to the hostile reaction this was likely to provoke in that country.

Then on 7 September the Chiefs of Staff revised their plans ('Musketeer Revise') by calling for the landings to take place at Port Said, further from Malta and Cyprus than Alexandria, and also for a preliminary air offensive before the landing to knock out the Egyptian air force and Egyptian military targets.

France, in an effort to hasten the operation, then contacted Israel at the beginning of September, in the expectation that her cooperation would help to deliver the *coup de grace* to Egypt. Israel, angered by Egyptian-backed terrorist attacks on her territory from the Sinai Desert, by the exclusion of her shipping from the Suez Canal on Nasser's orders and anxious to seize control of the Gulf of Aquaba to open Eilat as a major port for her trade, readily agreed to support the Anglo-French invasion. There then followed many weeks of clandestine meetings between French and Israeli officials, with Eden eventually agreeing to participate in the conspiracy. On 24 October, the French, British and Israelis signed the so-called Protocol of Sèvres, under the terms of which the Israelis agreed that they would seize the Sinai to the west of the Canal, which would then be followed by an Anglo-French ultimatum to both Israel and Egypt to withdraw their forces from both sides of the Canal. Israel would comply whereas it was anticipated that

Egypt would not: Anglo-French forces would then occupy the Canal after destroying the Egyptian air force.

President Eisenhower was not informed about these Anglo-French plans, although American intelligence was aware that something was going on. He made it clear that he would not support any forceful measures against Egypt; he was standing again for President in November and did not want such overseas complications to mar his campaign. However, Eden assumed that once the operation was under way the United States would acquiesce in the *fait accompli*. The efforts of Eisenhower's Secretary of State, John Foster Dulles, to suggest alternatives to the use of force, such as attempting to persuade Nasser to agree to the Canal being operated by an international users' consortium, were unsuccessful. Dulles hoped that negotiations to this end would impose a period of delay to allow passions to cool: Eden supported them, not because he believed that they had any prospect of success but because they would serve as a useful smokescreen while the Anglo-French build-up was being completed.

On 29 October Israel attacked and overran Egyptian positions in the Sinai Desert and soon approached the west bank of the Suez Canal. On 30 October Britain and France called for an immediate ceasefire and a withdrawal by both sides to ten miles from the Canal. When, as anticipated, Egypt rejected the ultimatum, a British bombing offensive destroyed 260 Egyptian aircraft, thus eliminating the Egyptian air force. The Soviets withdrew their planes and pilots from the battlefield. On 5 November Anglo-French parachute forces landed successfully at Port Fuad, while on the following day Anglo-French seaborne forces landed near Port Said and were soon moving towards the Canal. Altogether, the United Kingdom deployed 45,000 men, 300 aircraft and 100 warships during this operation.

The success of the invasion, after so much delay, did not bring much comfort to Eden, who now faced the concerted opposition of virtually all the members of the United Nations, with only lukewarm support for the invasion from Australia, New Zealand and South Africa. Furthermore, the Egyptians sank block ships in the Canal and also cut the oil pipeline to

Syria, an important source of Britain's fuel. While the Soviet Union threatened France and Britain with rocket attack and talked of sending Soviet 'volunteers' to help the Egyptians if the invasion was not called off, Britain faced even more serious opposition to her action from the United States. Eisenhower condemned the invasion out of hand, and her subsequent financial pressure caused the loss of 15 per cent of Britain's already meagre gold and dollar reserves in November alone, and the United States refused to support a British application for a loan from the International Monetary Fund until the British had withdrawn from Egypt. The Chancellor of the Exchequer, Harold Macmillan, recognizing that Britain faced financial ruin, and deeply concerned that the United States might also impose oil sanctions, at last called on Eden to abandon the enterprise. His intervention was decisive: the country was already deeply divided by the Suez adventure, while many senior Conservative Ministers were now opposed to continuing it.

On 2 November an emergency session of the United Nations General Assembly passed a resolution calling for a ceasefire in Egypt, the withdrawal of all foreign forces from Egyptian territory, the reopening of the Canal and the despatch of a United Nations force to the zone. Eden, warned by the Chiefs of Staff that the morale of the allied troops might disintegrate if a precipitate withdrawal was decided upon, hesitated for a time, leaving the Anglo-French forces stranded at Port Said, but eventually, to the fury of the French who were all for defying the United Nations, decided that the allies would have to give way. On 3 December Anglo-French forces began withdrawing from Egypt. The evacuation was completed by 22 December.

Conclusion

In 1950 British forces were actively involved in the Korean War as part of the United Nations' effort to defend South Korea against the North, and in 1956 British forces were again in action, this time in considerably greater strength as part of an Anglo-French effort to overthrow what they regarded as an anti-Western government in Egypt. During the years in between these two campaigns there had been little improvement in Britain's economic difficulties: an upturn in 1953 was followed by a recession in 1955. Britain's defence burdens remained as onerous as before 1950.

Some senior airmen were calling for reliance in future on the nuclear deterrent as a means of cutting expenditure on conventional forces, but this was strenuously opposed by vested interests in the army and navy and their associated defence industries. The shock to British pride resulting from her enforced withdrawal from Egypt in December 1956 enabled the supporters of nuclear deterrence to triumph over their opponents in 1957, when Britain adopted a strategy of massive retaliation on the same basis as that evolved by the Eisenhower Administration after 1953.

Notes

1 Truman subsequently denied that he had made the statement attributed to him.
2 Sir John Slessor, *Strategy for the West* (London, 1954).
3 I am grateful to Mr Martin Navias of King's College, London for allowing me to use this quotation.
4 Quoted in Stephen Kirby, 'Britain, NATO and European security', in J. Baylis (ed.) *British Defence Policy in a Changing World* (London, 1977), p. 104.

5 The Sandys White Paper and its Consequences, 1957–1963

The Sandys White Paper was the culmination of attempts since 1952 to reduce Britain's defence expenditure. The devastating financial and political consequences of the Suez Crisis in 1956 provided the impetus for a vigorous effort to achieve this. A determined Minister of Defence, with the full support of the Prime Minister, was able to overcome the formidable obstacles placed in his way by a well-entrenched service establishment and force through a programme which drastically reduced the size of Britain's conventional forces, and especially the army. Britain's possession of a growing nuclear arsenal provided Sandys with a convenient rationale for cuts which the government would have been required to introduce for financial reasons. Thereafter, the nuclear relationship between the United Kingdom and the United States assumed a dominant role in the partnership. All these developments took place against a background of continuing unrest in Britain's overseas possessions and spheres of influence. The drastic reductions in the size of the British Army made this unrest even more difficult to control after 1957.

The Sandys White Paper and the nuclear option

Early in January 1957, Eden, his health undermined by the strain of the previous few months, and having been discredited by the Suez débâcle, resigned and he was replaced as Prime Minister by Harold Macmillan who, ironically, had initially been a fervent supporter of the Suez invasion but at the last moment had turned against it. Macmillan was well aware of Britain's world-wide unpopularity as a result of the invasion. While Nasser had turned the ignominious defeat of his forces into a propaganda triumph, Britain's desperate financial predicament required her to mend her broken fences with the United States. The restoration of Britain's links with the United States and the Commonwealth, the recovery of her tarnished prestige and the salvaging of some vestiges of her influence in the Middle East after the recent humiliating retreat, would all take time. Meanwhile, however, urgent action had to be taken if Britain's economic difficulties were to be overcome; her gold and dollar reserves continued to fall during 1957.

The long drawn out preparations for the invasion, coupled with the shortages of equipment of every kind which those preparations had revealed, led Cabinet Ministers to question whether the large expenditures of the previous few years on conventional warfare capabilities had been money well spent. Certainly Macmillan, as a former Chancellor and Minister of Defence, was fully conversant with the difficulty of overcoming the entrenched resistance of the service lobbies to any major overhaul in British defence policy. On 13 January he appointed Duncan Sandys to the post of Minister of Defence, with instructions fundamentally to restructure Britain's armed forces, to rely in future on nuclear deterrence as the basis of Britain's defence posture and to secure 'a substantial reduction in expenditure and manpower'.[1]

Sandys was a forceful politician who would brook no opposition from the armed services to his sweeping programme of cuts, and he could rely, as no previous Minister of Defence had been able, on the full support of the Prime Minister for his measures, and both men were strong supporters of Britain's nuclear deterrent. Furthermore, in October 1955, Eden had strengthened the position of the Minister of Defence in the defence hierarchy by authorizing the Minister to take account of the composition and balance of Britain's armed forces, as well as of their cost. The Chiefs of Staff Committee was also provided with a permanent chairman; hitherto, the post had been held on a rotating basis by one of the chiefs who remained responsible at the same time for defending the interests of his own service. In 1957 the chairman was given the title of Chief of the Defence Staff (CDS), and Macmillan also increased Sandys's powers by creating a Defence Board consisting of the three service Ministers, the Chiefs of Staff, the CDS, the Chief Scientific Adviser to the Ministry of Defence and the Permanent Under-secretary at the Ministry, chaired by the Minister of Defence and which was intended to coordinate defence and service policies.

Lord Mountbatten, then First Sea Lord and Chief of the Naval Staff, described the experience of working with the autocratic Sandys as 'trying': they did, however, manage to work together sufficiently well to be able to impose their ideas on the rest of the defence establishment. In his White Paper *Defence: Outline of Future Policy*,[2] Sandys laid down the basis for Britain's future defence policy – 'it is ... in the true interests of defence that the claims of military expenditure should be considered in conjunction with the need to maintain the country's financial and economic strength' and that the way to reduce these claims would be for Britain to possess 'an appreciable element of nuclear deterrent power of her own'. In his White Paper[3] of the following year Sandys argued that there was 'no military reason why a world conflagration should not be prevented for another generation or more through the balancing fears of mutual annihilation. In fact there is no reason why this should not go on indefinitely ... when fully equipped with megaton weapons, the British bomber force will itself constitute a formidable deterrent.'[4]

Having based Britain's future defence firmly on nuclear deterrence, the rest of the White Paper defined the tasks of her conventional armed forces as 'to play their part *with the forces of Allied countries* in deterring and resisting aggression' and 'to defend British colonies ... against local attack and undertake limited operations in overseas emergencies'. Since allied forces were tending to become more integrated, Sandys insisted that it was no longer necessary for national forces to be 'self sufficient and balanced in all respects'. While Britain will 'provide her fair share' of the armed forces of the free world 'she cannot any longer continue to make a disproportionately large contribution.'[5] Britain would continue to assist Malaya's external defence after independence, defend the Persian Gulf and Aden and contribute two battalions to a Commonwealth Strategic Reserve based in Malaya and Singapore which she had agreed to set up with Australia and New Zealand in 1956. Defence expenditure was to be reduced from 10 to 7 per cent of GNP by 1962, with the budget being reduced by £180 million to a total of £1,420 million in 1957–8.

The consequences of this White Paper for the army were particularly severe. Conscription was to be abolished, being phased out by 1960. Total British armed forces manpower was to be reduced from 690,000 to 375,000 by 1962. The BAOR was to be cut from 77,000 men to 64,000 and the Second Tactical Air Force in Germany was to lose 220 day fighters. The introduction of tactical nuclear weapons would, in Sandys's view, amply compensate for these reductions. Overseas garrisons were to be pared down and withdrawn altogether, but a Central Army Reserve was to be set up in the United Kingdom which, provided with more modern transport aircraft, would be available for immediate action in the event of an overseas crisis. This idea had been discussed since the end of the Second World War, and had been mentioned in various Defence White Papers during the 1950s, but RAF Transport Command lacked suitable planes for the purpose of airlifting troops over long distances while the RAF, more interested in spending its money on V-bombers, had done little to remedy this situation, as the Suez operation planners had discovered. Nor was much done after 1957 to provide more and better quality planes.

The navy's future role in total war was briefly and ominously described as 'somewhat uncertain'. However, while the navy had already begun concentrating on improving its ability to intervene in limited conflicts by downgrading its global war mission, it had no intention of losing its aircraft carriers. Indeed, the navy argued that, with Sandys' decision to cut army garrisons overseas, the aircraft carrier would become even more important in helping to defend Britain's interests east of Suez. Thus, in future it proposed to station a carrier force permanently in the Indian Ocean. The future size of the fleet was to comprise three carriers, six cruisers, 55 destroyers and frigates and 32 submarines.

Clearly, the forthcoming testing of an air-dropped British hydrogen bomb in May 1957 and the coming into squadron service of the Vulcan bombers, capable of hitting Moscow, in the same year, enabled Sandys to emphasize the nuclear deterrent with greater confidence than his predecessors. While there was some evidence that the V-bomber squadrons might become more vulnerable to improved Soviet anti-aircraft defences by 1960, Sandys hoped to overcome this danger by authorizing the production of the British-built Blue Streak long-range intermediate, liquid-fuelled, unhardened ground-to-ground ballistic missile which would eventually replace manned aircraft altogether. Meanwhile, a stand-off airborne missile, the Blue Steel, was to be developed to prolong the life of the V-bombers by reducing their vulnerability to Soviet counter-measures. This enabled Sandys to cancel the production of a new manned supersonic bomber.

There was not a great deal that was new in Sandys's White Paper, which was the culmination of thinking about nuclear deterrence in British defence policy-making circles since the early 1950s. Ending conscription had also been on the political agenda for some time: it was electorally unpopular and was not considered to be a very effective or efficient way of securing the steadily rising requirement of skilled manpower for the increasing technologically complex weapons systems which were entering the inventories of the armed services.

While the cuts which Sandys imposed were regarded as drastic at the time, no thought at all was given to reducing the considerable array of commitments with which Britain had been encumbered since 1945 and which had necessitated the re-introduction of national service and a large sea-going navy in the first place. Indeed, Sandys insisted that Britain would adhere to all her existing defence obligations in the Middle and Far East. Britain was faced with a number of colonial and post-colonial crises after 1957 and she was hard put at times to find the manpower and equipment to deal with them: if they had all occurred at the same time, she would have been faced with a very serious situation. As it was, the army frequently complained that with the 165,000 men Sandys had forecast would be its maximum size in 1962 (this was subsequently increased to 180,000), it would be unable to cope. Furthermore, in the aftermath of the Suez Crisis, many Arab and Asian countries had refused to allow Britain the right to overfly or land on their soil. In 1957, Ceylon forced Britain to abandon the use of the Trincomalee naval base. This led the British government to develop the island of Gan in the Maldives as an air staging base, and to consider building up Kenya as a base for British troop concentrations in the event of troubles arising in the Middle East or Africa. Some £3.5 million were spent on improving the garrison facilities in Kenya before the Colonial Secretary, Ian Macleod, suddenly decided in 1960 that Kenya should be given its independence.

Nuclear deterrence was regarded as a means of obtaining a capability for defence and retaliation on the cheap, while Britain's insistence on remaining an independent nuclear power compensated to some extent for the loss of her *amour propre* in November 1956. The RAF believed that it would provide a useful adjunct to the US Strategic Air Command in the event of a nuclear war with the Soviet Union: indeed, the RAF would be able to bomb targets in the USSR which the United States did not feel to be essential to their plans while, if the United States, faced after 1960 with a Soviet retaliatory capability, refused to come to the assistance of Western Europe in an emergency for fear that her towns and cities would then come under attack, Britain would have the ability to act independently against the Soviet Union. Consideration was also given at this time to sending nuclear weapons to Singapore for SEATO purposes and to stockpile them in Cyprus for the defence of the CENTO area.

None of these calculations was fulfilled. Nuclear deterrence was destined to become a commitment of ever increasing expense as new and more sophisticated missile systems were developed more frequently. It soon became beyond Britain's financial and technological capability to produce these weapons herself and she was forced after 1960 to buy them more cheaply from the United States. Thus, her 1957 notion of future nuclear independence proved to be illusory except in the short run and the Cabinet even in 1957 had doubted that Britain would ever use them unilaterally. In 1960 Britain insisted on the right to employ her American-produced missiles independently in an emergency, but it was extremely unlikely that she would do so. To add to her difficulties, the stocks of conventional warfare equipment left over from the rearmament programme of the Korean War were, by the end of the 1950s, either used up or obsolescent and a major re-equipment effort would be required in the near future.

The revival of the Anglo-American nuclear relationship, 1957-1960

Skilful diplomacy by Macmillan did at least lead to the restoration of Britain's close ties with the United States. The Prime Minister met Eisenhower at Bermuda in March 1957 and agreed to the stationing of 60 American Thor IRBMs on British soil, under a dual-key firing arrangement. In return, Eisenhower at a further meeting with Macmillan in Washington in October 1957 promised that he would press Congress to agree to the full renewal of exchanges of nuclear information which had been brought to such a sudden end in 1947. Collaboration had in fact been renewed in 1954, after Britain's successful Monte Bello test explosion of the atomic bomb, when the Eisenhower Administration had persuaded Congress to pass the Atomic Energy Act which allowed for the transfer of information to Britain on the size, shape, weight and yields of her atomic bombs. The 1958 Anglo-American Agreement for Cooperation on the Uses of Atomic Energy for Mutual Defence Purposes of 3 July 1958 led to the complete restoration of nuclear information exchanges between the two countries. Britain could now learn the latest developments in American engineering and weapons assembly, while the United States found that Britain had advanced beyond them in other fields of nuclear research.

Nor did the cooperation between the two countries end there. In April 1960 the British government cancelled Blue Streak. With development costs mounting, the slow-to-fire weapon required at least 15 minutes warning of a Soviet attack before it could be airborne: the joint Anglo-American Ballistic Missile Early Warning System (BMEWS) which had been set up at Fylingdales on the Yorkshire Moors only gave Britain four minutes advance warning of a Soviet salvo. To replace it, Harold Watkinson, Sandys's successor as Minister of Defence, purchased 100 Skybolt air-to-ground missiles from the United States in June 1960. This purchase had been agreed at a meeting between Eisenhower and Macmillan in Washington in March. The United States was to provide the missile, while the United Kingdom manufactured the warheads. This could be fired by V-bombers at a long distance from target, thus making the Vulcans even less vulnerable to Soviet anti-aircraft defences than if they were equipped with Blue Steel missiles. The government hoped that this would enable the V-bomber force to remain operational until the early 1970s.

While this decision enabled the United Kingdom to acquire nuclear weapons from the United States at a much reduced cost to her exchequer than if she had produced them herself, it inevitably entailed her increasing dependence on the United States, contrary to the intention behind the 1957 White Paper that the British deterrent should be a genuinely independent one. The 1961 and 1962 White Papers stated that Britain's nuclear missiles would 'trigger the United States' deterrent', which suggested that Britain was now less than confident about her ability to counter the Soviet Union on her own. However, the purchase of missiles direct from the United States enabled Britain to achieve substantial long-run savings, since the United States had to bear the heavy research and development costs involved in producing them. In the early 1960s, however, the cancellation of her obsolescent home-produced weapons meant that she had to write off her development costs although, on the other hand, the abandonment of Blue Streak saved her about £500 million in future expenditure.

The TSR-2

The problems Britain encountered in a rapidly changing technological environment, where existing weapons systems were soon replaced by new and more advanced types, were not of course confined to long-range missiles, but they were the most expensive items in the inventory. During the 1960s, the cost of new weapons of all kinds began to increase much faster than the rate of inflation. For instance, new destroyers capable of firing missiles cost twice as much as the large pre-Second World War battleships (£28 million against £14 million). The consequences of these escalating costs were much more severe for Britain than for the United States, with her massive resources and large-scale defence industries. The United States was, of course, as anxious as the United Kingdom to restrain the growth of her defence expenditure, but Britain's deteriorating economy, and her narrow military industrial base, made her search for economies more urgent. The abandonment of national service and the attempt in 1957 to replace manpower by weaponry in the future was part of a long-run trend towards more capital-intensive methods of waging war. Britain soon discovered that the savings she had anticipated from this process in 1957 did not materialize and thus her financial problems worsened in the following decade.

Pressures in both the United States and Britain to reduce the growing number of highly specialized single-purpose weapons led their respective defence departments to call for the production of multi-role combat vehicles which could be deployed for more than one purpose and by more than one armed service. This applied particularly to the field of aviation, where the rate of obsolescence resulting from successive qualitative innovations was much greater than for other weapons and where the navy and air force were competing to obtain aircraft for use in a single theatre or for a particular strategic role. Thus, the Ministry of Defence sought to procure one aircraft which could perform two or more roles, thus achieving savings in procurement costs and the benefits of economies of scale from the production of a larger number of multi-role planes. This resulted in the development in the United States and Britain of a number of multi-role prototypes which, because of the sophistication and complexity of the various tasks they were supposed to meet, could not achieve any of them satisfactorily without expensive modifications, and even then their efficiency was not guaranteed.

An example of this was the ill-fated British TSR-2 strike and reconnaissance aircraft. After 1957 the Air Staff began to search for a replacement for the Valiant bomber and for the Canberra fighter bomber. The Canberra was then being deployed by the Second Tactical Air Force in West Germany. It seemed to make financial sense to develop a plane which could be used to perform the two roles previously performed singly by the Valiant and Canberra respectively. Thus began the saga of the TSR-2, which was intended to have a 1,000 mile radius for missions east of Suez, where it was to be capable of flying at high speeds and at high altitudes, and to be capable of being used for army cooperation purposes in Europe flying at low speeds at low altitudes with a 600 yard take-off capability. Research on this plane began in the late 1950s, but already by 1962 the Treasury was becoming alarmed by the huge cost overruns and the slow progress of this project.

This did not lead to the cancellation of the TSR-2. Designers, engineers, civil servants and politicians alike were naturally reluctant to admit that their previous assumptions about the viability and cost-effectiveness of this plane had been inaccurate, and to write off the large sums that had already been invested in the project. They continued to hope that once its teething troubles had been overcome, an efficient aircraft would emerge.

The purchase of Polaris from the United States, 1962

The problems which soon caused the Skybolt missile to be cancelled were another example of the unwillingness of politicians to admit that their original enthusiasm for a project had been misplaced. Its purchase had been authorized by Macmillan and Watkinson based on the technical advice which was available to them at the time. The United States Air Force was already fully committed to a weapon which would perpetuate its strategic nuclear monopoly, and strongly recommended Skybolt to the Royal Air Force. Thus, the RAF would also be able to maintain its sole control over the British nuclear deterrent while the American and British air forces could cooperate in the selection and apportioning of targets in the Soviet Union.

The Americans had begun research and development on a submarine-launched, long-range ballistic missile, Polaris, in the early 1950s and it would be deployed in the early 1960s. Eisenhower offered this to the United Kingdom as an alternative to Skybolt. The Admiralty was not enthusiastic about this missile, fearing that it would cost so much that the navy would be forced to sacrifice some of its other missions, and it had no intention of losing its aircraft carriers.

Information reaching the Ministry of Defence from the United States that Skybolt was running into increasing technical difficulties and cost overruns was ignored. When John F. Kennedy became President of the United States in 1961 he appointed a cost-conscious statistician, Robert S. McNamara, to the post of Defense Secretary. McNamara wanted to reduce the growing number of missile systems which were being developed in the United States and to concentrate instead on procuring the second generation solid-fuelled Minuteman land-based ICBMs and the Polaris sea-launched ICBMs. One of the first victims of his economy drive was the Skybolt missile, which he cancelled on 7 November 1962.

This was a severe blow to Britain's nuclear pretensions. McNamara regarded the possession by medium-rank powers like Britain and France of their own independent nuclear weapons as unnecessary and dangerous in a volatile strategic environment. Both he and Kennedy wanted Britain to abandon her nuclear role and concentrate instead on building up her conventional forces in Western Europe to strengthen NATO's land defences so that they would be able to 'force a pause' on the Soviet Union if she attacked Western Europe and thus allow time for negotiations before nuclear weapons were deployed by either side.[6]

Macmillan hurriedly arranged to meet Kennedy at Nassau in the Bahamas between 20 and 22 December where he complained bitterly about the cancellation of Skybolt and demanded that the United States provide a substitute. The fervour with which the Prime Minister put his case so impressed Kennedy that he agreed to supply Britain with an alternative. Furthermore, the Americans feared that if Britain was not given some satisfaction in the matter, she might abandon NATO. Already, General de Gaulle, who had become leader of France in 1958, was creating difficulties for the United States, demanding an enhanced status for France in NATO, and Kennedy had no wish to antagonize his British ally whose loyalty to NATO had never previously been questioned. There was some discussion that Britain might take over Skybolt from the United States and develop it herself, but this was likely to be beyond her resources especially as valuable American expertise would no longer be available to her. Macmillan therefore accepted Kennedy's offer of Polaris in return for a promise that Britain would assign the new weapon to NATO, although Macmillan reserved the right to use it independently in the event of an emergency arising when NATO either could not or would not act.

This decision confirmed Britain's status as a nuclear power for the foreseeable future. Nevertheless, the notion of her nuclear 'independence' was becoming increasingly threadbare given her reliance on the United States for warheads and the American assistance that would subsequently be required for servicing and modernizing the system. This situation suggested that Britain would not launch the missile without prior American agreement. Britain's nuclear role tended to complicate strategic planning, increase her financial difficulties and result in growing internal dissent.

Developments in Britain's defence policy, 1960–1963

In 1959 the size of the BAOR was further reduced to 55,000 men. Britain again claimed that enhanced tactical nuclear fire power would make up for this loss of manpower, and argued that in any case the withdrawal of her troops was necessitated by the increasing expense of maintaining her forces in West

Germany. Since West Germany had ceased to be an occupied power in 1955, having recovered her sovereignty in that year by agreement with the United States, France and Britain, the British could no longer charge the costs of the BAOR to the West German exchequer, as she had been entitled to do under the occupation regime. The British Treasury estimated that the BAOR was costing Britain about £50 million a year in the late 1950s which would rise to about £75 million by 1960. Long negotiations between Britain and West Germany led eventually to West German agreement to alleviate Britain's financial burden by paying her £12 million a year in support costs from 1958 to 1962, but this, of course, met only a small proportion of the total cost.

In 1960, Britain caused her NATO allies considerable irritation when she announced that she would have again to reduce the size of the BAOR to 49,000 men. However, this was not implemented following strong West German protests and when European tension rose after 1960 when Khrushchev threatened to turn over control of the access routes from West Berlin to the East German authorities unless the Western allies agreed to evacuate their sectors of the city and sign a peace treaty with the German Democratic Republic. Kennedy insisted that the West would stand firm on her rights in the city. He placed American forces on full alert in 1961 and recalled American reservists to the colours as a warning to Khrushchev not to interfere with the West's access to Berlin. Britain agreed therefore not to reduce her forces in West Germany any further and promised to maintain them at the 1959 level of 55,000 men. Finally, an offer by West Germany to increase the size of her contribution towards the BAOR's support costs eased Britain's financial problems in Europe.

The decision not to cut the size of her army in West Germany any further went against Sandys's assumption in 1957 that her possession of nuclear weapons would enable Britain progressively to reduce her conventional forces and which had led to the abandonment of conscription in 1957. Sandys himself was beginning to have doubts about this policy by 1959. Harold Watkinson, who replaced him as Defence Minister in September 1959, concluded that Britain had allowed her land

and sea forces to deteriorate too much given that they were so essential to the maintenance of her numerous overseas responsibilities.

Watkinson had served in the Royal Naval Volunteer Reserve during the Second World War and sympathized with the navy's case for more resources. The Chief of the Defence Staff, Lord Mountbatten (1959–1965), the First Sea Lord, Sir Charles Lambe, and Sir Solly Zuckerman, the Chief Scientific Adviser at the Ministry of Defence, were also enthusiastic navalists and worked together to improve the navy's seaborne and carrier-borne forces, with Watkinson's full approval. Zuckerman also believed that Britain should rely on cheaper American nuclear weapons than on her own production, and use the money saved for conventional purposes.

New commando carriers, assault and supply ships were ordered for the navy after 1959, but no decision was taken about replacing the older aircraft carriers, *Hermes*, *Victorious*, *Ark Royal* and *Eagle*, although Watkinson agreed that these should be modernized. In 1960 Britain had two fleets west of Suez (one in the Mediterranean and the other in the Atlantic), while east of Suez she had a large Far East fleet at Singapore. There were also frigates located in the Persian Gulf and at the Simonstown naval base in South Africa. The Chiefs of Staff also approved the development of Aden as the future 'springboard' for the defence of British interests in the Middle East and the Indian Ocean. Considerable sums of money were invested in the provision of new docks, air strips and barracks at Aden in the belief that Britain would remain in the colony for at least 25 years. However, nationalist disturbances broke out there in 1963, leading the services to question the value of Aden as a secure British base.

A number of overseas emergencies requiring the deployment of British troops and naval forces in these years reinforced the effort to improve Britain's conventional forces. On the other hand, there was some reduction in Britain's commitments. British forces evacuated Jordan in 1957, while a revolution in Iraq by a group of nationalist and anti-British army officers in October 1958 forced Britain to abandon her two air bases there. A temporary settlement of the Cyprus conflict was achieved in 1959 when, at a conference in London attended by Britain, Greece, Turkey and representatives of the Greek and Turkish Cypriot communities, it was agreed that Cyprus should become independent with a Greek Cypriot President and a Turkish Vice-president. Britain was to retain two 'sovereign base areas' on the island to contain 6,000 of her servicemen (the Cyprus emergency had tied up 25,000 British troops before 1959).

However, to set against these reductions in Britain's responsibilities, she had to provide troops to deal with a number of crises which occurred elsewhere. Until 1959 she had provided British ground and air support to the Sultan of Muscat and Oman to help him contain a tribal revolt which was supported by Saudi Arabia. In 1957, Britain accepted responsibility for the external defence of Malaya when she granted that country her independence, and in the following year this protection was extended to Singapore. In 1958, British troops were airlifted to Jordan to help the King maintain order following Egyptian-inspired unrest against the monarchy. In July 1961 a British task force was despatched to Kuwait (source of 50 per cent of Britain's oil supplies) to defend the country against a threatened Iraqi takeover, which in the event did not materialize. In 1964, troops were flown to Kenya, Uganda and Tanganyika to help their governments crush army mutinies. From 1963 to 1967 British ground, air and naval forces were engaged in a sustained campaign to thwart Indonesia's efforts to undermine the newly created Federation of Malaysia comprising Malaya, Singapore, Sabah (North Borneo) and Sarawak.

The 'confrontation' with Indonesia over-extended Britain's forces, and if a major crisis had broken out elsewhere at that time Britain would have found herself unable to deal with it. The central reserve of rapid intervention forces which had been promised in the 1957 White Paper had not been set up owing to financial restrictions which had prevented the purchase of new transport planes and other equipment. Watkinson accordingly allocated £80 million in his 1959 and 1962 budgets for this purpose.

His 1961 and 1962 White Papers called for 'balanced forces'

so that NATO could be provided with a capacity for graduated deterrence which would enable the West to parry a Soviet attack with conventional forces in the first stages of a conflict. However, Watkinson's successor, Peter Thorneycroft, believed that nuclear weapons would be employed earlier in such a war and was not prepared to devote as much money to NATO's conventional forces. In any case, Britain's role east of Suez was becoming more pronounced; an average of 100,000 service personnel were based there after 1960. The 1963 Defence White Paper emphasized the importance to Britain of her commitments in Arabia and the Persian Gulf and of her contribution towards 'the containment of Communism' in South East Asia. Thorneycroft hoped that defence expenditure could be stabilized at £1,800 million per annum (7 per cent of GNP), with the total armed forces standing at 400,000 men, for the rest of the decade.

Conclusion

The decision in the 1957 Defence White Paper that Britain would in future rely only on nuclear deterrence for her future defence was scarcely a revolutionary step: it had been discussed widely in British defence circles from the early 1950s and was the logical culmination of the 1946 Cabinet decision to produce a British atomic bomb. The adoption of massive retaliation by the United States had enabled the Eisenhower Administration to reduce considerably the size of America's conventional forces, and thus it seemed an attractive proposition to Britain's leaders, anxious to reduce the heavy burden of defence expenditure in the aftermath of the Suez débâcle. Publicly, Britain's nuclear deterrent was proclaimed to be a truly 'independent' weapon which Britain would manufacture and deploy by herself. Privately, the Cabinet in 1957 appreciated that it could not be used except in cooperation with the United States and, given the mounting costs of the delivery systems, which were beyond Britain's capacity, this had to be admitted when during and after 1960 Britain was forced to purchase Polaris and Skybolt missiles from the United States.

The truly 'independent' British deterrent only lasted for three years.

Nor did the decision lead to any real alleviation of Britain's defence problems since the government did not contemplate any reduction in Britain's overseas commitments. She was faced with meeting the same obligations after 1957 as before, but now with less manpower and in a steadily deteriorating economic climate. The mismatch between resources and liabilities was settled to some extent in 1968 by her retreat from her role east of Suez, but this was by no means a foregone conclusion in 1960.

Notes

1 Quoted in Philip Darby, *British Defence Policy East of Suez, 1947-1968* (Oxford, 1973), p. 107.
2 *Defence: Outline of Future Policy* (London, HMSO, Cmd 124, April 1957).
3 *Report on Defence: Britain's Contribution to Peace and Security* (London, HMSO, Cmd 363, February 1958).
4 Quoted by A. J. R. Groom, 'The British deterrent', in J. Baylis (ed.) *British Defence Policy in a Changing World* (London, 1977), p. 27.
5 Quotations from Sir Richard Powell, 'The evolution of British defence policy', in G. Frank, M. Imber and J. Simpson (eds) *Perspectives upon British Defence Policy 1945-70* (Proceedings of a Ministry of Defence Conference held at Winchester in April 1975), pp. 44-5, 51.
6 Quoted in C. J. Bartlett, *The Long Retreat: a Short History of British Defence Policy, 1945-1970* (London, 1972), p. 158.

6 The End of Britain's Role East of Suez, 1964–1968

Despite the reductions in the size of Britain's conventional forces that had taken place in 1957, the defence estimates resumed their upward path in the early 1960s. The Sandys White Paper had barely made any impression on the size of Britain's overseas commitments, which increased in number and intensity in these years. Dependence on nuclear deterrence as the main weapon in Britain's armoury proved to be increasingly expensive and to have no relevance to the low-intensity conflicts in which the British were engaged in the Persian Gulf and against Indonesia.

Nevertheless, Harold Wilson's Labour government after 1964 attempted to hold down defence expenditure and at the same time cling on to Britain's role east of Suez. Wilson's effort to square the circle came to grief in 1967–8 when a succession of serious financial and economic crises forced the goverment to abandon its role east of Suez and concentrate its defence efforts on the West European theatre. The previous Conservative government had sought to associate the country economically with Western Europe in 1963 when it had applied to join the European Economic Community. Both this application and one by the Wilson government in 1967 were rebuffed by France. Britain therefore turned its attention to the strengthening of the NATO alliance as if to demonstrate its new-found commitment to West European defence and security.

The Labour government and defence: the role east of Suez 1964–1968

With its defeat in the General Election of October 1964, the long period of Conservative government came to an end. Its record in the field of defence had been a rather uneven one. Although the bulk of Britain's colonies had achieved, or were on the point of achieving, their independence, this has led to little more than marginal reductions in her overseas commitments, which were almost as extensive in 1961 as they had been in 1951. The forces that were available to her to fulfil her European and overseas liabilities had, however, been drastically reduced in size as a result of the Sandys White Paper of 1957, but this did not occur because of any fundamental change in Britain's strategic situation but had been forced on her by financial and economic necessity. The decision to place more emphasis on nuclear deterrence and less on conventional arms was a response to continuing balance of payments deficits and the resulting outflow of her gold and dollar reserves, made worse by American sanctions during the Suez Crisis, a last ditch Anglo-French effort to keep their privileged positions in the Middle East and North Africa.

However, reliance on nuclear deterrence for her defence did not result in any long-term alleviation of her financial difficulties, contrary to the reasoning behind the 1957 White Paper. The mounting costs of warheads and delivery systems forced Britain to abandon the idea of an independent nuclear force in favour of reliance on cheaper American technology. Real economies could only have been achieved in this period if Britain had contemplated sweeping reductions in her overseas commitments and concentrated her resources on the defence of Western Europe, but this was never seriously considered by the leading figures in either the Conservative or the Labour Party. The failure to bring her defence commitments into line with her straitened resources exacerbated her economic difficulties during the 1960s, and the resulting strains forced the Labour government into a headlong retreat from Britain's responsibilities outside Europe.

Nor were Britain's European NATO allies greatly impressed by her claim that the enhanced firepower provided by tactical nuclear weapons would more than compensate for reductions in the BAOR. This argument aroused fears in Britain and elsewhere in Europe that West Germany might press for the right to acquire her own nuclear weapons on the grounds that Britain's failure to live up to her 1954 promise to keep four divisions of troops in Europe had deprived West Germany of adequate defence. These fears were shared by members of the Labour Party, many of whom remained suspicious of West Germany. Other members of the Party had been influenced by the Campaign for Nuclear Disarmament (CND). CND demanded not only that Britain renounce the possession of nuclear weapons, but also that she give a lead to other countries by forming an international non-nuclear club. The belief that other countries would follow suit if Britain abandoned her nuclear deterrent was another example of the widely held assumption that Britain occupied a unique position of moral leadership in the world.

The movement for unilateral nuclear disarmament created deep divisions in the Labour movement. There was an outcry when Aneurin Bevan, widely considered to be a unilateralist, told the Brighton Labour Party Conference in October 1957 that without the independent nuclear deterrent Britain's influence in the world would disappear. He called on the Conference to reject a resolution repudiating Britain's possession of nuclear weapons otherwise 'you will send a Foreign Secretary, whoever he may be, naked into the conference chamber.'[1] In fact, Bevan was more concerned that without the deterrent Britain would become an American satellite, and that West Germany might acquire nuclear weapons if Britain abandoned them. The growing support for nuclear disarmament in both the United States and Britain, which was fuelled by growing anxiety about the genetic and other consequences of the fallout from nuclear tests by the United States, the Soviet Union and Britain during the 1950s, led the Labour Party to campaign during the 1959 General Election for the setting up of a non-nuclear club.

Labour's defeat in 1959 led to further convulsions within the

Party over the nuclear issue. The Party leader, Hugh Gaitskell, was convinced that Britain must keep her nuclear deterrent as an insurance in case the United States abandoned her nuclear protection of Western Europe, or if the Soviet Union came to believe that the United States would stand aside from a conflict between the West Europeans and the Warsaw Pact. He accepted that Britain might reduce or even abandon her nuclear deterrent if a genuine multilateral nuclear arms agreement was negotiated, but this would have to include guarantees for the future security of all states. He promised that a future Labour government would work to achieve such an agreement. He faced considerable opposition to this policy from within the Party, and especially from some of the powerful trade union leaders, and at the Party Conference at Blackpool in 1960 there was a large majority in favour of Britain's unilateral nuclear disarmament. After strenuous efforts, Gaitskell managed to get this resolution reversed at the Party Conference the following year; in the meantime, Khrushchev's threats about Berlin had turned many erstwhile supporters away from unilateralism, while the appeal of the CND was beginning to decline.

After Gaitskell's sudden death in 1962, Harold Wilson, considered to be on the left wing of the Party and sympathetic to the unilateralist cause, was elected leader. When he eventually led the Party into office in October 1964 with a majority of five MPs his future policy on the nuclear issue and on defence in general was by no means clear. The government was committed to multilateral disarmament and to remaining in NATO, although Wilson had tried to appeal to nuclear disarmers during the election campaign by talking vaguely of the need to renegotiate the Nassau agreement on the Polaris missile. While this threat alarmed the Americans, Wilson never spelled out what his intentions were and the matter remained dormant after 1964.

In fact, the defence policies of the new Labour government differed hardly at all from that of its Conservative predecessor. A meeting of the new Cabinet at the Prime Minister's official country home, Chequers, on the weekend of 21 and 22 November, confirmed that Britain would retain the independent nuclear deterrent, although Ministers agreed that it would not be replaced when its useful life came to an end. Since the cancellation of the order for Polaris would involve Britain in considerable severance payments to the United States, this decision was hardly an unexpected one. This Cabinet meeting also resolved that Britain would maintain her role east of Suez and, as far as Wilson was concerned, this became an article of faith for the next four years.

There was thus much continuity in the defence and foreign policies of the Conservative and Labour governments of this period. Both believed that Britain still had an important role to play in the Middle and Far East. The Conservative Defence White Paper of 1964 stated that 'In Asia and Africa, in all the under-developed regions, there are powerful forces for change and it is for us both an interest and a responsibility to help it to take place with a minimum of violence.'[2] The Wilson government made the similar claim that her forces overseas were Britain's contribution to international peace and security.

Wilson thought that the Commonwealth was still a viable concern, and an important source of trade and investment opportunities for Britain. Its survival depended on the continuation of Britain's overseas defence role. The 1965 Defence White Paper even suggested that the BAOR might be further reduced in size in view of the reduced threat from the Soviet Union and that the resources thus saved could be used to increase the strength of Britain's forces east of Suez. He faced increasing criticism from Labour backbenchers about these overseas pretensions but he reiterated to the House of Commons on 16 December 1964 that 'I want to make it quite clear that ... we cannot afford to relinquish our world role.'[3]

The argument for remaining east of Suez was reinforced by Wilson's concern for the continuation of Britain's 'special relationship' with the United States, which he believed would be fatally compromised if Britain withdrew her forces from Hong Kong, Malaysia and the Persian Gulf. Both John F. Kennedy and his successor Lyndon B. Johnson expressed their appreciation for Britain's role east of Suez, fearing that if Britain abandoned it there would be increasing instability and tension there. Wilson alluded to these fears in 1965 when he asked 'Who would replace us?' There were also the traditional arguments that Britain's military and naval presence in these regions was essential if her vital supplies of oil and raw materials and her trade and investments were to be protected. That Japan's burgeoning trade in the Far East was not disadvantaged by her lack of bases or an ocean-going fleet was overlooked in Whitehall.

No detailed investigations were undertaken to test the validity of these assumptions, which were based on tradition and wishful thinking rather than on any empirical evidence. Britain's experiences after 1970, when she had largely abandoned her world role, suggested that the presence of British forces east of Suez had not contributed much to the maintenance of her commercial interests there or to her international prestige. Her declining economy was a much more telling indicator of her real strength, and the presence of a few battalions of troops, naval vessels and airplanes in distant parts of the world did little to improve this. The Commonwealth had never been a particularly harmonious or united grouping even in its heyday. When it had consisted entirely of white self-governing dominions it had come to the assistance of the motherland during the two world wars but, given the increasing dependence of its members on the United States' financial and military strength and the steady growth of more inward-looking and less anglocentric attitudes on the part of its various populations, it was even less inclined to follow Britain's lead after 1960 than it had been before. South Africa withdrew from the Commonwealth in 1962. Moreover, the Commonwealth became increasingly diversified in religious, racial, political and economic terms after 1947 and in the late 1950s and early 1960s when Britain granted independence to most of its remaining colonies. This was not an organization which had anything in common except a shared memory of British rule. During the 1960s, trade between Britain and her Commonwealth partners began to decline as its members developed their own industries and regional trading arrangements. This was another factor which pushed the United Kingdom closer to Europe, its major customer, after 1968.

The other arguments for the continuation of Britain's role east of Suez were also shown to have been considerably exaggerated during the 1960s. Although Kennedy closely consulted Britain during the 1962 Cuban missile crisis and Britain played a leading part in the negotiations for a test ban treaty in 1963, her influence on the United States waned after 1965, a result of her continuing economic decline and Wilson's refusal to send British troops to assist the United States in Vietnam. Britain's overseas role gave her no influence at all on America's policy in Vietnam.

Denis Healey as Secretary for Defence, 1964–1970

Wilson chose as his Defence Secretary, Denis Healey, one of the few Labour politicians who had taken much interest in defence and foreign affairs and who had the strong personality necessary if he was to impose his will on the vested interests in his Department. He was to occupy the post for six years, the longest tenure since it was created in 1947. Healey's task was assisted by the administrative reforms Peter Thorneycroft had imposed on the defence establishment during his short period as Minister between 1963 and 1964. The Chief of the Defence Staff, Mountbatten, was a keen advocate of defence centralization and in this he had been supported by Thorneycroft, a former Chancellor of the Exchequer, who was aware of the possible economies which would result from the reorganization and modernization of the defence establishment. In January 1963, Thorneycroft had invited Lord Ismay and Sir Ian Jacob to propose reforms, and their report of 20 February was the basis of the government's subsequent plans, which were put into effect on 1 April 1964. The Minister of Defence now became Secretary of State in a unified structure, with three Ministers of Defence under him for the navy, RAF and army. The First Lord of the Admiralty and the other service Secretaries of State were abolished, while the former Board of Admiralty and Army and Air Councils became sub-committees of the Defence Council for individual service matters. This Council was chaired by the new Secretary of State and its membership included the three Ministers of Defence, the Chiefs of Staff, the CDS, the Permanent Under-secretary at the

Department of Defence and the Chief Scientific Adviser. The Cabinet Defence Committee now became the Defence and Overseas Policy Committee. This reorganization was not, of course, popular with the armed services since it would considerably reduce their autonomy.

In the early 1960s efforts were made to restructure Britain's defences overseas; commands were rationalized and unified so that by 1962 there were only three: the Near East Command based at Cyprus, the Middle East Command based at Aden, and the Far East Command based at Singapore.

Healey shared Wilson's belief in the importance of Britain's role east of Suez (on a visit to Canberra in February 1966 he insisted that 'we have no intention of ratting on any of our commitments')[4] and of Britain's nuclear deterrent. He was not a supporter of close links with Europe. He was impressed by the need to bring defence expenditure under control (he described the defence budget as 'a runaway train')[5] and in November the Cabinet ordered its reduction to £2,000 million per annum at 1964 prices until the financial year 1969–70, i.e. 6 per cent of GNP instead of the 8.3 per cent it had reached under the Conservatives. As inflation increased, Healey's task became increasingly difficult, especially as Britain's armed forces required extensive modernization, despite the improvements that the Conservatives had ordered during their last years in power. Furthermore, some of the Third World countries with whom Britain might have to contend during the 1960s, like Iraq and Indonesia, were rearming their forces with increasingly sophisticated technological equipment, and while they might lack the skilled personnel to operate this effectively it was a problem Britain would increasingly have to face if she maintained her overseas role.

The Soviet Union was also improving the quality of her conventional military material during the 1960s and this was bound to lead to increasing American pressure on Britain and the other NATO allies to update their armed forces. However, none of these countries was prepared to make the sacrifices in domestic living standards that would be required for this purpose, any more than they had been during the 1950s. The parliaments and public opinion of these countries were more interested in defence economies and in increased expenditure on social welfare, and this applied especially to a British Labour government which prided itself on its concern for the well-being of the people. Public and press tended to take a more relaxed attitude to the Soviet threat than their governments, especially in Britain, where the USSR remained a remote country.

No doubt Britain could have kept her world role indefinitely if this had been the only way of preserving her vital interests and if she had been prepared to devote more resources to the task. Since 1945, successive governments had been committed to full employment and the welfare state. At least until the 1980s governments tried to improve social conditions and any suggestion that welfare provision should be cut back significantly was a recipe for political suicide. Peter Thorneycroft had resigned as Chancellor of the Exchequer in 1958 when the Cabinet had rejected his proposals for reductions in such expenditure. Even when Britain had been faced with a more serious and a more direct threat to her security from Nazi Germany in the 1930s than that posed to her by the Soviet Union after 1947, and when social welfare provisions were much more rudimentary, she had been reluctant to embark on full-scale rearmament until 1939.

As it was, Britain's defence expenditure as a percentage of her GNP after 1947 averaged 6 per cent a year, by contrast with an average of about 3 per cent between 1933 and 1938. This represented a considerable achievement given her economic difficulties. Nevertheless, defence slipped to third place in national expenditure behind education and the National Health Service. This imposed intolerable burdens on her economy, leading to a fall in investment in manufacturing industry and creating inflation as the public and private sectors competed for skilled labour and raw materials. The British people faced the inconvenience of rationing and other restrictions on personal expenditure until the early 1950s, which was the consequence of their government's decision to cling to Britain's overseas role. Under these circumstances it was scarcely surprising that Britain became increasingly unable to compete on equal terms with her competitors in the world market and that her balance of payments fell further into deficit, a situation which was made worse by the heavy foreign exchange costs of her overseas commitments.

Britain's defence problems, 1964–1966

By the mid-1960s orders placed by the Conservatives for new self-propelled artillery, armoured infantry carriers, cross-country vehicles and rockets were being delivered to the BAOR. The Chieftain tank, better armed and armoured than the Centurion, was now being deployed, but the army lacked new helicopters and other new weapons and Healey could not authorize expenditure on these without breaching the Cabinet's expenditure limits.

Even while they were striving to maintain Britain's world role, Wilson and Healey were forced by each successive financial crisis to withdraw from bases and commitments which they had only shortly before insisted were essential. The 1965 White Paper referred to the increasing strains of Britain's defence efforts but made no suggestions as to how these might be alleviated: indeed, it praised Britain's unique peace-keeping mission. A fifth Polaris submarine which the Conservatives had ordered was cancelled on the grounds of the shortage of skilled labour. The Royal Navy, which was becoming the most expensive of the three services, would have to make do with four. Replacements for the Hunter and a medium transport aircraft were also cancelled.

The decision which caused the most uproar was Healey's cancellation of the TSR-2 on 6 April 1965 at a saving of £300 million in the financial year, on the grounds of its escalating cost and poor prospects. The abandonment of the TSR-2 did not diminish Healey's enthusiasm for Britain's role east of Suez: he announced that 50 American FB-111A fighter bombers were to be purchased at £380 million each, with 12 being used for extra-European operations to replace the Canberra for long-range bombing and reconnaissance. He claimed that the FB-111s would perform these tasks more cheaply than the TSR-2 and would enable him to keep the estimates at the £2,000 million level. Healey believed that the FB-111 could be used to replace the Royal Navy's expensive carrier-borne aircraft provided sufficient air bases were available to the RAF east of Suez. (Britain had developed the island of Gan in the Indian Ocean as an air staging base after the Ceylon government refused to allow Britain to use her base at Trincomalee.)

Healey now insisted that Britain would not become involved in major military operations overseas without the cooperation of her allies, thus hinting at economies in the navy's amphibious warfare capability. Accordingly, Healey cancelled a new aircraft carrier (VA01) whose development he had authorized in 1965, and while he approved the refitting of the carrier *Ark Royal* and agreed that the navy could keep all four older carriers in commission until 1975, he made it clear that they would not be replaced. This led to an outcry from the naval establishment and to strong protests from the Conservatives, but neither these nor the resignation of the Minister of Defence for the Navy, Christopher Mayhew, and the First Sea Lord, Admiral David Luce, caused him to change his mind. The White Paper insisted that such economies would enable the government to plan for a viable defence posture in the 1970s, one which would continue the deployment of her forces world wide.

The FB-111A was also intended to bridge the gap between the demise of the Canberra and the entry into operation of a variable geometry strike and reconnaissance aircraft, which the British and French were to develop jointly. Given the expense involved for one country in the production of a multi-role aircraft, it seemed sensible to encourage joint developments of this kind. It was assumed that each participating country would make substantial savings and the wasteful proliferation of designs would end. Such collaboration with Britain's European allies was also encouraged by Whitehall since it demonstrated Britain's increasing identification with her continental neighbours and would at the same time allow for the survival of Britain's aircraft industries which might otherwise be unable to compete with their American counterparts in world markets.

However, in the same way that dual or tri-service projects led to friction and increasing expense as each service sought to load the prototype with its own operational requirements, so too each country insisted that such projects conformed to its own strategic and tactical needs. There was also intense competition to try to ensure that each country's aircraft manufacturers secured a fair share of the work. Given all these problems, many of these projects foundered. The Anglo-French variable geometry plane was abandoned when talks between the two countries broke down in 1967. The same fate was nearly shared by the Tornado multi-role combat aircraft which the RAF wanted for high-speed low-level operations in the 1970s. It was agreed in 1967 that this should be produced by the United Kingdom, West Germany and Italy. It had therefore to perform a number of specialized roles to meet the requirements of each of these countries:

Long-range strike and interdiction (enemy movements and communications): for Britain and West Germany
Land-based strike at maritime targets: for Britain and West Germany
Close support of ground forces on battlefield: for Britain (secondary role) and Italy
Air superiority: West Germany (secondary role) and Italy
Reconnaissance: Britain
Air defence interception: Britain
Training: Britain, West Germany and Italy[6]

Britain's share of the cost was to be £4,000 million, and she was to take 385 of these machines. It was hoped that they would be operational in the 1970s. Endless delays and cost overruns meant that they did not become available until the 1980s.

Britain's retreat from her role east of Suez, 1966–1968

A serious economic crisis in July 1966 began the process which was to lead to the end of the east of Suez strategy. Opposition to that role in the Labour Party was increasing in intensity. While the Defence White Paper of February 1967 asserted that no drastic changes were contemplated, the writing was already on the wall. In 1966, Britain had announced her intention of evacuating strife-torn Aden when South Arabia became independent in 1968. Nor would Britain agree to defend South Arabia thereafter. However, she insisted that she would maintain her other commitments in the Persian Gulf, and indeed would slightly increase the size of her naval forces there. In April 1967, with the end of the confrontation between Malaysia and Indonesia, 10,000 British servicemen were withdrawn from Borneo.

During the late 1960s both the Commonwealth ideal and the usefulness of Britain's overseas role as a means of defending her commercial interests came under increasing criticism as a result of two overseas crises: Rhodesia's unilateral declaration of independence in November 1965, and Britain's inability to persuade Israel to give up her conquests after the 1967 Arab–Israeli War.

Prolonged Anglo-Rhodesian negotiations had failed to resolve the issue of Britain's insistence that before Rhodesia could be granted her independence the black African majority in Rhodesia must be given the same voting rights as the white minority. The white minority wished to preserve its special position in Rhodesian society and political life, and while its leaders were prepared to make a few concessions to the blacks, these in no way met Westminster's requirements. When the negotiations collapsed in November, the white Rhodesian government severed its links with the British Crown and declared its independence on 11 November. Further negotiations after UDI with the Rhodesian Prime Minister, Ian Smith, broke down over the central issue of black representation. Britain was unwilling to impose a settlement by force. This affair was a considerable set-back for Britain's standing in the eyes of many Commonwealth members, particularly among the black African states. Rhodesia was a British colony, yet Britain was unable or unwilling to take any measures to force the illegal white minority regime to give way.

A supplementary Defence White Paper on 18 July 1967 represented the Wilson government's final admission that financial and political realities had made the sacrifice of the major part of Britain's responsibilities east of Suez inevitable.[7] Her armed forces in Singapore and Malaysia were to be reduced by 50 per cent by 1971, and they were to be withdrawn completely between 1975 and 1977. Aden was to be evacuated immediately, although a British naval force was to remain in the Persian Gulf. RAF and naval air transport were to be cut back, thus abandoning the Conservative government's central reserve capable of dealing with overseas emergencies quickly. These reductions enabled the government to reduce the defence estimates by £300 million by 1970 and to cut service manpower by 75,000 over the same period. Healey stated that his Ministry would conduct a 'continuing ... review' of overseas spending and service manpower to see where further economies could be made.

This seemed even more necessary when on 18 November 1967 another financial crisis forced the government to devalue sterling and as a result Britain's overseas defence bill increased by £50 million. The government imposed reductions on all public expenditure, with a further £100 million to be taken from the defence budget during the 1967-8 financial year. This led to the speeding up of the 1967 timetable for the withdrawal from east of Suez. On 16 January 1968 Harold Wilson announced that all British forces were to be withdrawn from Malaysia and Singapore by 31 March 1971 (although this was later extended to December 1971), and all Britain's aircraft carriers were to be scrapped by 1971. The order for the 50 FB-111As was cancelled. Britain would in future maintain only small garrisons in Hong Kong, Gibraltar, Belize and the Falkland Islands.

The final stage of Britain's 'long retreat' from empire was accomplished with considerable haste. The dire consequences to Britain's trade and investment that many politicians and civil servants had predicted would result failed to materialize. Britain had not accepted in 1947 that, with India's independence, the rationale for Britain's continued presence in the Middle East had been removed. Again, during the 1960s, Britain's leaders had failed to come to terms with the fact that her policy of rapid decolonization had made her overseas military role superfluous, while it had not given her the means to influence events.

The 1968 cut-backs meant that in future Britain would concentrate her resources on the defence of Europe and on the nuclear deterrent. Her willingness to become more closely involved in the affairs of Europe was further emphasized when, in December 1967, the British government applied to join the European Economic Community, which had been established by the six main continental powers in 1955. Then Britain, firmly wedded to free trade, the Commonwealth and her world role, had refused to associate herself with the Community. Her application in 1967 was vetoed by President de Gaulle, whose policies during the 1960s sought to free France and Western Europe from United States' domination and who claimed *inter alia* that if Britain joined the EEC she would, because of her close links with the United States, merely be the spokesman for American interests.

In 1966 France had withdrawn her military forces from NATO on the grounds that it was merely the vehicle for American control of Western Europe and, although France retained her political links with the Alliance, she expelled SHAPE from her territory (it moved to Mons near Brussels). The United States had rejected French demands for a share in nuclear decision-making, insisting that only the President of the United States could authorize the employment of the deterrent. France had started to develop her own atomic bomb in the 1950s and had tested her first atomic bomb in 1962. The French airborne nuclear deterrent (the *force de frappe*) was intended to assert France's independence from the so-called Anglo-American bloc.

Ironically, at the same time, Britain was beginning to take a new interest in NATO. The French withdrawal had weakened the military capability of NATO at a time when the other members were reducing their force levels. Furthermore, the combat readiness of the American army in Europe was weakened by the transfer of its better-trained troops to Vietnam during the 1960s and their replacement by raw conscripts. Later in the decade, the demoralization which began to affect American troops in Vietnam spread to the American army in

Europe, thus further weakening its military credibility. In the face of these difficulties, Healey after 1967 worked to inject a new sense of coherence and purpose into NATO's organization and planning. In December 1967 he persuaded the NATO Council of Ministers to adopt the strategy of flexible response to Soviet aggression. This decision in effect enabled each NATO member to determine the kinds of forces it wanted to contribute to SHAPE. McNamara had been trying without success to get NATO to adopt this strategy.

In August 1968 Warsaw Pact forces invaded Czechoslovakia to crush Czechoslovak government moves to assert its independence from the Soviet Union. The shock effects of this action on Western Europe led the Nato Council in September to call on its members to increase the size of their armed forces. The Soviet move was a reminder to the West that the Soviet Union was prepared to act ruthlessly to protect its interests. Healey promised that more money would be devoted to the improvement of the quality of the BAOR's military equipment.

Washington failed to consult Britain or her other European allies about her decision to enter into strategic arms limitation talks with the Soviet Union which began at Helsinki on 17 November 1969. The Europeans feared that the United States might reach agreements with Moscow which would weaken extended deterrence and which would otherwise affect their security interests. Wilson and Healey encouraged the setting up of a ten-nation Eurogroup within NATO which was intended to apply concerted pressure on the United States to keep Europe informed about the talks. Healey now spoke of an increased 'European defence identity'.

Conclusion

The Labour government's 1968 decision to withdraw from east of Suez was forced on the Wilson government by a series of economic and financial crises, each one more serious than the last. In November 1967, two months before Wilson announced the decision, Goronwy Roberts, a Foreign Office Minister, assured Britain's Persian Gulf allies that she had no intention of withdrawing her forces from the region.

The nuclear deterrent was thus shown to be largely irrelevant to the global defence problems with which Britain was faced before 1970: she could hardly threaten to use the hydrogen bomb against Indonesia or Iraq. Nor had the deterrent produced the economies in defence expenditure that Sandys had anticipated and, this being the case, the next logical step was the abandonment of the bulk of Britain's overseas responsibilities. It took eight years before this was achieved, a result of Wilson's determination to cling to Britain's role east of Suez despite the growing opposition from the Labour Party and mounting evidence that it was not producing the expected benefits. Britain's financial problems were alleviated by the decision to withdraw, but they were certainly not solved. During the next decade and a half she continued to be faced with the problem of reconciling her means to her less extensive but still onerous ends.

Notes

1 Quoted in John Campbell, *Nye Bevan and the Mirage of British Socialism* (London, 1987), p. 339.
2 Quoted in Philip Darby, *British Defence Policy East of Suez, 1947–1968* (Oxford, 1973), p. 240.
3 Ibid., p. 284.
4 Ibid., p. 296.
5 Quoted in C. J. Bartlett, *The Long Retreat: a Short History of British Defence Policy, 1945–1970* (London, 1972), p. 170.
6 Dan Smith, *The Defence of the Realm in the 1980s* (London, 1980), p. 133. Reproduced by kind permission of Mr Dan Smith.
7 Ministry of Defence, *Supplementary Statement on Defence Policy* (London, HMSO, Cmd 3357, 1967).

7 Britain's Defence Problems in the 1970s

This chapter is concerned with Britain's adjustment to her transition from a global to a regional power. This process did not, however, cause her to undertake any new efforts to strengthen her forces on the Continent, and indeed by the mid-1970s much of the equipment of her armed forces needed replacing or up-dating. During the Wilson administration (1974–6) expenditure on defence declined in real terms while the government concentrated its resources on improving welfare and social security provisions. After 1977, however, the Callaghan government began to repair the worst deficiencies in the weapons of the BAOR and RAF Germany. It agreed to spend an additional 3 per cent of GNP on defence annually for the following five years. In the meantime, the British Army found itself faced with another internal security problem, not in some outpost of Empire, but nearer home, in Northern Ireland. The civil conflict in the Province threatened to saddle the army with a continuing commitment.

The Northern Ireland question

In June 1970 the Labour Party was defeated at the General Election and a Conservative administration under Edward Heath came into office. Since the Conservatives had last held power Britain's defence posture had been completely transformed. The major part of Britain's defence efforts were now directed to NATO and her extra-European commitments, apart from a few garrisons, were on the point of being liquidated. However, in 1969 the British army became closely involved in the internal security problems of Northern Ireland. During the late 1960s, Northern Ireland was plunged into increasing turmoil as a civil rights movement campaigned against the discrimination of the Roman Catholic minority in the province by the Protestant-dominated Northern Ireland government. Frequent clashes occurred between demonstrators and Protestant gangs, with the Royal Ulster Constabulary (RUC) poised uneasily between the two. When the situation threatened to get out of hand, the Northern Ireland government decided to call out the 'B' Specials, a reserve force composed of mainly Protestant volunteers, to assist the increasingly beleaguered RUC. Fearing that the use of this force would only provoke further protest and violence, the British government decided to send in British Army units to take over the security of the province. The Catholic population in Northern Ireland at first welcomed the British troops but relations soon turned sour after they were forced to intervene to restore order when demonstrations got out of hand. Inevitably, Catholics suffered assaults from the security forces during such mêlées and feelings became inflamed. When some British paratroopers fired on a Catholic crowd on Bloody Sunday in 1972, killing 13 and wounding other demonstrators, relations between the Catholics and the British army deteriorated further.

After 1970, the British army struggled to contain a rising tide of violence, much of which was engineered by a terrorist organization, the Irish Republican Army (IRA), which sought to create such turmoil in the province that either the province became ungovernable or the British population on the mainland would tire of the long drawn out struggle and demand the withdrawal of British troops from Northern Ireland. The IRA hoped that the result would be the establishment of an all-Irish Republic of Eire and Northern Ireland. IRA terror provoked counter-terror from Ulster Protestant extremists (the so-called Ulster Defence Association) with the Northern Ireland population, both Catholic and Protestant, the victims of their activities.

In 1972, the British government suspended the constitution of Northern Ireland and imposed direct rule from London. The Northern Ireland government had not appeared to be very enthusiastic about promoting political and other reforms which would have given the Roman Catholics more equality, and it was in any case too closely identified with the Protestant majority. Various proposals were put forward during the 1970s by the London government for constitutional changes which would give both communities an equal voice in the government of the province – such as the sharing of power between the two communities – but these foundered on the opposition of one side or the other. Thus, the British army was faced with the seemingly endless task of policing the province and the resulting strain on army manpower forced the Ministry of Defence to transfer troops (almost a division during the 1970s) from the BAOR to Northern Ireland.

Edward Heath and defence policy

When Heath entered office in 1970 the responsibility for Britain's nuclear deterrence had been taken over entirely by the Royal Navy, whose four nuclear submarines, *Resolution*, *Renown*, *Repulse* and *Revenge*, were now patrolling the high seas. The Vulcan B2 medium bomber continued to be deployed by the RAF, but the main task for the RAF was now the provision of theatre and tactical support for NATO's ground force with the Vulcans and Buccaneers. These were to be replaced by the Jaguar ground attack fighter, a joint Anglo-French venture, after 1975.

While in opposition, the Conservatives had vigorously attacked Labour's abandonment of Britain's role east of Suez, and had promised that if they were elected in 1970 they would restore some of these overseas commitments. In practice, this did not amount to very much. Heath was more firmly committed to Western Europe than any of his predecessors at No. 10 Downing Street. In January 1972 he secured Britain's entry into the EEC, de Gaulle having been replaced as French President by Georges Pompidou who was more sympathetic to

Britain's application. Except for important cooperation in nuclear research and intelligence gathering, the 'special relationship' with the United States now had little meaning. President Richard Nixon concentrated on extricating the United States from the war in Vietnam, on pursuing *détente* with the Soviet Union and on establishing diplomatic relations with Communist China. Under these circumstances, Europe tended to be neglected by the United States. During the early 1970s relations between America and Europe reached their lowest point since the end of the Second World War.

Heath was angered by American support for Pakistan during the 1971 Indo-Pakistan war, which drove India further into the arms of the Soviet Union. Then there was an even more serious rift between the United States and her European allies over their respective policies towards the Arabs and Israelis during the Middle East war of October 1973. American support for Israel ran into the opposition of most of the West European states, who wanted to safeguard their vital oil supplies from the Middle East by taking a more sympathetic line towards the Arabs than they had during previous Middle Eastern conflicts. Saudi Arabia took the lead in the Organization of Arab Petroleum Exporting Countries (OPEC) in imposing quotas on the export of oil to force non-Arab countries to change their policies. Until 1967, the oil-importing countries had been able to purchase their oil supplies fairly cheaply: now restrictions on the production and export of oil caused prices to rise by a dramatic 70 per cent, imposing vastly increased costs on West European industries, costs which Britain in particular could ill afford to bear.

In an effort to appease the Arab states, West European countries (except The Netherlands) refused to allow American air force transport planes flying military supplies to Israel to load or even land on their airfields, while Nixon's order on 25 October 1973 of a world-wide defence alert of American forces without first consulting his European allies created considerable friction. However, these incidents, although regarded as serious at the time, caused no lasting damage to relations between Europe and the United States.

A supplementary Defence White Paper issued in the

summer of 1970 by the Defence Secretary, Lord Carrington, confirmed that the Heath government would continue its predecessor's European-orientated defence policy virtually unchanged. In December, the Cabinet approved a NATO proposal for a European Defence Improvement Scheme which would require Britain to spend £400 million over the next three years on updating BAOR equipment. However, some of the extra-European commitments which Wilson had abandoned were restored. Britain would continue to contribute forces to an ANZUK (Australia, United Kingdom and New Zealand) land, sea and air force in Malaysia and Singapore. The United States and Britain were to build a joint naval base on Diego Garcia in the British Indian Ocean Territory. The 1955 Simonstown agreement with South Africa which allowed the naval base to be used by the Royal Navy was to be reactivated in view of the importance of keeping the Cape route open to Britain's trade. The government agreed in return that arms supplies to South Africa, which had been suspended by the Wilson government as a reaction to South Africa's racialist policies, would be resumed. The aircraft carrier *Ark Royal* was to be kept in commission until 1978. In April 1973, the government authorized the construction of through-deck or anti-submarine warfare (ASW) cruisers, virtually small aircraft carriers, each capable of carrying five Sea Harrier vertical take-off and landing (VTOL) jets, carrying air-to-air guided missiles, and ten ASW helicopters. The first, *Invincible*, was launched in 1977. They were intended to provide the Royal Navy with an air component into the 1980s. The third such cruiser was named *Ark Royal* after the original aircraft carrier. While more British forces were to be assigned to the Central Treaty Organization, Britain's naval withdrawal from the Persian Gulf took place in 1971 as planned.

The Wilson government had concluded by the end of the 1960s that Britain's financial and economic strength was of greater importance to her international standing than her presence east of Suez and that excessive expenditure on defence was self-defeating since it undermined Britain's economic base while adding little to her security or prestige. Heath believed that Wilson had gone too far in cutting the defence budget and had, as a result, made a coherent defence policy difficult to achieve. He felt that the economy could stand a slight increase in defence expenditure from Wilson's goal of 5 per cent of GNP from 1968 to 1973 to 5.75 per cent of GNP. Heath hoped that this level could be maintained over a long period. This increase enabled him to promise that there would be no change in the current strengths of the regular army and Territorial Army.

The Labour government and defence, 1974–1979

In February 1974, the Heath government was defeated at a General Election which the Prime Minister had called in the face of a national coal strike. The Labour Party was returned to office with a small minority, with Harold Wilson again Prime Minister. The oil price increase and the coal strike had plunged the balance of payments once again into deficit and, with unemployment rising, the economy was faltering. The Labour Party had, during the election, promised the electorate that if it was returned to power it would undertake major improvements in social welfare provision. In this period, the cost of new military equipment was increasing faster than inflation. Dan Smith has calculated that the proportion of the defence budget spent on military equipment rose from 35 per cent in the early 1970s to 41 per cent in the late 1970s, while the proportion spent on manpower declined from 47 to 42 per cent during the same period.

The decision to abandon Britain's role east of Suez in 1968 had not resulted in a substantial alleviation in defence expenditure, although if it had not taken place the financial situation would have been even more serious in the 1970s than it was. Roy Mason, the Secretary of Defence from 1974 to 1976, was concerned that advances in weapons technology would result in the defence budget rising to 11.25 per cent of GNP after 1979 unless remedial action were taken.

These dismal estimates resulted in a new Defence Review in December 1974 which called for a new round of defence cuts. Defence expenditure was to be reduced from a level of 5.5 per cent of GNP in 1975 to 4.4 per cent by 1985, a figure of £3,300 million at 1974 prices. As a result, savings of £4.75 billion over the ten-year period were anticipated. 'Clear strategic priority areas' were identified, which entailed the abandonment of many of the extra commitments which Heath had undertaken:

1 The NATO Central Front in West Germany, where it was intended to keep the BAOR at a strength of 55,000 men, and Second Tactical Air Force at its existing size.
2 The defence of the Eastern Atlantic and the English Channel.
3 The defence of the United Kingdom and its approaches.
4 The maintenance of the strategic nuclear deterrent, although Labour promised that it would not be replaced when it became obsolete. Britain's tactical nuclear capability was also to be retained.

The navy bore the brunt of the cuts in equipment and weaponry, losing one-seventh of its surface combat fleet, while its presence in the Mediterranean was reduced to a small force of anti-submarine vessels. These reductions took place at a time when Royal Navy fishery protection vessels were under considerable strain in trying to defend British fishermen during the 'Cod War' with Iceland, resulting from the latter's extension of her territorial waters which affected Britain's traditional fishing grounds in the North Sea. There were to be major reductions in the Royal Air Force's transport fleet, while amphibious and airborne forces were also to be cut back. The armed forces were to shed 11 per cent of their existing manpower, about 38,000 men, by 1979, while British army garrisons in the few remaining overseas possessions were to be substantially reduced. The planned effects are given in table 7.1.

The Defence Review declared that these sacrifices were essential if resources were to be released for investment in civilian industries and if the balance of payments was to be improved. It also made the familiar complaints that Britain was undertaking more than her fair share of the burden of defence by comparison with her NATO allies and that, as a result, her trading competitors were given a decided advantage.

Table 7.1 Actual manpower in April 1974 and that planned for April 1979 in the three armed services, and their respective percentage reductions

	April 1974	April 1979	%
Royal Navy and Marines	79,000	74,000	−6
Army	180,000	165,000	−8
RAF	100,000	83,000	−18

Source: Keith Hartley, 'Defence with less money? The British experience', in Gwyn Harries-Jenkins (ed.), *Armed Forces and the Welfare Societies: Challenges in the 1980s* (London, 1982), p. 20. Reproduced by kind permission of Dr Hartley.

The Defence White Paper of March 1975 called for further reductions to bring expenditure down to 4.5 per cent of GNP over the ten years to 1985, with further cuts in troop levels and the withdrawal of all British naval vessels from the Mediterranean. That these reductions were justified seemed to be confirmed when sterling collapsed again in 1976. A direct protest from the Chiefs of Staff to the Prime Minister about the destabilizing effects of the cuts upon the armed services was ignored.

The Labour government kept expenditure on the nuclear deterrent at between 1 and 2 per cent of GNP after 1974. However, Wilson was faced with the problem that the effectiveness of the Polaris fleet would decline markedly by the end of the decade, and Labour had promised not to replace it. By 1975 the United States would have ended the production of Polaris missiles and replaced them by the Poseidon submarine-launched ballistic missile, with multiple independently targetable re-entry vehicles, which could strike at a large range of targets after launching. This was considered to be too sophisticated for British deterrent purposes.

The Heath government had, shortly before it fell from power, recommended that the British Polaris system should be modernized to provide it with multiple warheads which could be manoeuvred in space, and which would be equipped with decoys to confuse enemy anti-missile defences. The Wilson government adopted this recommendation. Like the original decision in 1947 to produce an atomic bomb, a small group of senior Ministers chaired by Harold Wilson authorized 'Project Chevaline', as the modernization programme was described, and once again this was concealed from Parliament by charging the cost (£1,000 million by 1980, well above the original estimate) to the maintenance budget.

Project Chevaline was made possible as a result of British underground testing of the new missiles in Nevada between 1974 and 1976, an indication that the Anglo-American 'special relationship' was still very much alive in the nuclear field at least. Furthermore, the 1972 Anti-Ballistic Missile Treaty signed by the United States and the Soviet Union had left the Soviet Union's cities (except Moscow) vulnerable to missile attack from third powers like Britain and France. Chevaline enabled the government to put off consideration of a new generation of submarine-launched nuclear missiles until the 1980s.

The programme of defence cuts continued until 1977. In 1976, following the sterling crisis, Britain announced that she would no longer contribute to the ANZUK force in Singapore. She also terminated the Simonstown Agreement with South Africa, and closed down the Gan air staging base in the Indian Ocean. In future, Britain's overseas responsibilities were confined to Gibraltar, Cyprus, Hong Kong, Belize and the Falkland Islands (see table 7.2).

Roy Mason was replaced as Minister of Defence by Frederick Mulley in October 1976. While Mason had been Defence Secretary he and the other NATO Defence Ministers had been under increasing pressure by Supreme Allied Commander Europe (SACEUR) to do something to improve NATO's defences. These had been neglected during and after 1970 chiefly as a result of the improvement in East–West relations resulting from *détente*. However, towards the end of the decade *détente* began to falter, as suspicions grew in the United States that the Soviet Union had taken advantage of the Strategic Arms Limitation Agreements, and of the anti-military

Table 7.2 British forces deployed outside NATO, 1979

	Army	Royal Navy	RAF
Antarctica		Ice patrol ship	
Belize	1⅔ infantry battlions	Frigate	Harrier aircraft Puma helicopters and Rapier missiles
Brunei	1 gurkha infantry battalion		
Diego Garcia		Naval party	
The Falklands		Royal marine detachment	
Hong Kong	3 Gurkha infantry battalions and 1 British infantry battalion	5 patrol craft	Helicopters

Source: Dan Smith, *The Defence of the Realm in the 1980s* (London, 1980), p. 116.

feeling that had swept the United States in the aftermath of the Vietnam War, to improve the quality of her nuclear and conventional forces. Soviet interference in a number of Third World conflicts and her invasion of Afghanistan in December 1979 persuaded many Americans that *détente* had produced no real change in Soviet hostility towards the West, while Republicans accused the Carter Administration of complacency in the face of the increasing Soviet threat to American interests.

As a result of these developments, NATO adopted a major expenditure programme on the re-equipment and expansion of its forces by 3 per cent per annum over the following five years. James Callaghan, who replaced Harold Wilson as Prime Minister in 1977, agreed to this commitment in the expectation that it could be paid for from the proceeds of the oil revenues generated by the exploitation of Britain's North Sea oil reserves, development of which had become profitable as a result of the swingeing increases in oil prices at the beginning of the decade. He promised that there would be no further reductions in army manpower, that more tactical missiles would be procured for the RAF, while 41 Commando units, scheduled for disbandment, would be retained.

This increased expenditure was urgently needed. The BAOR's equipment required replacement or modernization. The army wanted a new tank to replace the Chieftain, and in September 1978 ordered the Main Battle Tank 80 (MBT 80) which, fitted with Chobham armour, was better defended than its predecessor. These would cost £1 million each, three times as much as the Chieftain tank. New artillery was also required. However, equipment problems were not the only shortcomings affecting the armed services in the late 1970s. Shortage of manpower, especially skilled manpower, was preventing many naval vessels and aircraft from being deployed effectively, while cut-backs in oil supplies and other economies meant that exercises had to be cancelled at short notice.

The manpower shortages stemmed from the inadequacies of service pay, made worse by the escalating cost of living. As a result recruits fell off, particularly for the skilled trades, where more lucrative employment could be found in the civilian sector. Officers on short-term engagements were not renewing their commissions when their time expired, and there was a large increase in the number of officers seeking early discharge. There were rumours that many soldiers were taking part-time jobs in their spare time ('moonlighting') and reports of increasing demoralization. In April the Armed Forces Pay Review Body stated that the pay rates of the armed services had fallen 30 per cent behind those in similar civilian trades. The Callaghan government, facing a wave of industrial unrest in 1978, was reluctant to concede a large pay increase to the armed services fearing that this would open the floodgates to a wave of claims from the civilian sector of the economy. In the end, pressure from the Chiefs of Staff and growing resentment in the armed services forced Callaghan to agree to a three-stage award of 13 per cent from 1 April 1978, and further increases over the next two years which would bring the total to 30 per cent. The Chiefs of Staff did not think that this would be sufficient: they argued for the whole sum to be paid at once.

Conclusion

The 1970s were years of relative stagnation in Britain's defences. The Heath government (1970–4) made some minor gestures towards fulfilling its election promises about restoring Britain's role east of Suez, but it was more concerned with entering the European Economic Community than with global issues. The ensuing Labour government soon abandoned the few overseas commitments Heath had entered into. Defence issues tended to be neglected, apart from the decision to proceed with Project Chevaline. After 1977, recognition that the armed forces were in urgent need of modernization, coupled with evidence of increasing Soviet hostility towards Western interests, led Britain and her allies to agree to devote an additional 3 per cent of their resources to improving NATO's defence posture down to 1986. Moreover, Britain's armed services were showing signs of increasing demoralization towards the end of the decade as a result of the erosion of pay by severe inflation, and it soon became clear that salary increases would have to be accepted if the capability of the services was not to be adversely affected. While the retreat from empire in 1968 had solved some of Britain's defence problems, the cost of new technology and weapons was spiralling by the end of the 1970s and the incoming Conservative administration was forced to make further adjustments to the defence budget.

8 The Thatcher Government and Defence, 1979–1988

Discussion of the Thatcher government's record in the field of defence has inevitably been dominated by the Falklands War of 1982. There is already a huge bibliography attempting to explain and analyse all aspects of this conflict: its causes, its course and its consequences. There is not sufficient space available here to attempt more than a cursory examination of that war (but see Further Reading section for details of two fuller accounts).

The Battle for the Falkland Islands was a dramatic exception to Britain's post-1968 policy of concentrating almost all her defence efforts on Western Europe and NATO. Indeed, in 1981, when the Thatcher administration was faced with the necessity of imposing further economies on the armed forces, it shrank from the politically hazardous course of reducing the size of the BAOR and RAF Germany. This would have excited strong condemnation from the other NATO countries and would have undoubtedly contributed to the internal pressure in the United States to bring American troops home from Europe.

Instead, the government chose to sacrifice a considerable proportion of the Royal Navy's surface fleet. This, it was believed, would have less impact on NATO than army reductions. These reductions had not become effective by 1982 which enabled the services to prepare and deploy a formidable task force in March and April 1982. If Argentina had waited a further year or two, Britain would have found it impossible to find sufficient carriers, landing and other vessels even to attempt the recapture of the islands.

As a result of the Falklands War, the government rescinded the bulk of the economies it had imposed on the navy in 1981. However, the continuation of the rise in the costs of advanced technology and the decision to purchase a new generation of nuclear warheads from the United States makes the government's expressed determination to maintain the present size of Britain's conventional forces a questionable one.

British defence policy, 1979–1982

The General Election of May 1979 returned the Conservative Party to Parliament, with Mrs Margaret Thatcher as Prime Minister. In their election campaign the Conservatives had promised to make greater efforts than the Labour government in improving Britain's defences and had talked of reviving some of Britain's former commitments outside Europe. One of the government's first decisions was to award an immediate pay settlement to the armed forces of 33 per cent. However, the effects of the world depression on the British economy, the imposition of tight monetary controls on public expenditure and the remorseless rise in the cost of new weapons forced the Defence Secretary, Francis Pym, to abandon all thought of increasing defence expenditure. There could be no question of a return to an overseas role, even in the limited way Heath had attempted in 1974. Nor was it clear that the government would agree to continue the commitment of the Callaghan government to spend an extra 3 per cent in real terms for NATO purposes until 1986.

At the same time, the government found itself faced with increasing criticism from nuclear disarmers about its predecessor's agreement to the basing of 96 cruise missiles at American air bases in Britain. In fact, several NATO countries had requested the United States to base these missiles in Western Europe in 1979, as a counter to Soviet emplacements of medium-range SS20 nuclear missiles in Central Europe. The cruise missile is a low-flying, relatively slow weapon which, following the contours of the earth's surface, can evade enemy radar. It has a range of 1,750 miles. The Federal

Republic of Germany accepted Pershing II missiles, while the cruise missiles in Britain were divided between Greenham Common and Molesworth air bases in 1983. The wave of protest against these new missiles in Western Europe was echoed in Britain by the revival of the Campaign for Nuclear Disarmament which fostered public demonstrations against the American missiles, while a number of women camped outside the gates of the Greenham Common air base to gain publicity for the anti-nuclear cause.

The Thatcher government was as unlikely to be swayed by this kind of pressure as it was by similar protests when it decided to replace Polaris by a new generation of submarine-launched ballistic missiles. Polaris was ageing and the Americans were already developing a new system, the Lockheed Trident C4 SSBN, for the 1990s, which President Carter offered to sell to Britain in December 1979. This was more accurate and reliable than Polaris, equally invulnerable and with longer ranges.

On 15 July 1980 the Thatcher government announced its intention of purchasing Trident at a cost of £5 billion which was to be spread over the following ten years, working out at about 3.5 per cent of the total budget during that period and 6 per cent of the equipment budget. Some defence analysts thought that this projection was too low: that the costs would in fact amount to about 7.5 per cent of the defence budget down to 1993. The government has recently announced that the costs will be even less than the £5 billion it originally estimated as a result of savings in construction costs and lower inflation in the United Kingdom. Britain will build the four new nuclear submarines, providing about 13,000 jobs for the workforce in Barrow-in-Furness and other shipyards, while the United States will supply 13 Trident missiles for each boat, and each missile will have 8 MIRVed warheads.

A complication arose in 1981 when the United States decided to substitute a new missile, the D5, for the C4, which would have greatly improved range, accuracy and more warheads. This degree of sophistication was probably out of all proportion to what Britain required, but the government's difficulty was that the United States would have phased out production of the C4 before Britain would need the missiles. The government therefore had little alternative but to accept the D5. In a new document, *The United Kingdom Trident Programme* issued in March 1982,[1] the government announced that the D5 'offered greater commonality with the United States' system through its projected service life. This would give us continued assurance of weapon system reliability without the large investment programme which would be required to provide an equivalent degree of assurance with a weapon system unique to the United Kingdom.'[2]

The government's plans therefore went ahead with complete disregard for the activities of the Campaign for Nuclear Disarmament. The Labour Party, however, could not ignore CND pressure. Many of the Party's members were members of CND, while others were strongly influenced by its anti-nuclear propaganda. In 1982, the Party adopted a fully fledged unilateralist platform, calling for the withdrawal of all American bases and missiles from British soil and the abandonment of the British nuclear deterrent. However, the Party did endorse Britain's continued membership of NATO, but with the provision of conventional forces only to the alliance.

The government embarked on an effort to reduce defence expenditure after 1980 by seeking savings in administrative costs and through greater efficiency in the armed services through the Management Information System for Ministers and Top Management, and by introducing more competitive tendering into the procurement process. But this is unlikely to yield more than marginal savings. When Francis Pym failed to demonstrate sufficient energy in imposing reforms on the services, Mrs Thatcher replaced him in 1981 by John Nott, who was more committed to the government's monetarist programme. He was faced with the problem that, given that Britain's nuclear deterrent was to be renewed, there were only two areas where economies could be made: in the BAOR in West Germany or in the size of Britain's surface fleet, which provided about 70 per cent of NATO's naval capabilities. Given the fear that any reduction in the BAOR would encourage the United States to reduce its force levels in West

Germany, it was regarded by the Ministry of Defence as politically inexpedient to tamper with Britain's contribution to continental defence. As a result, John Nott's Defence Review, *The United Kingdom Defence Programme: the Way Forward*, opted instead for cuts in Britain's surface fleet as a course likely to cause less overseas criticism than reductions in the army.[3] He admitted that 'even the increased resources we plan to allocate to defence cannot adequately fund all the force structures and plans for their improvement we now have.'[4] As a result, in future the Royal Navy was to concentrate on its nuclear deterrent role and on anti-submarine warfare. The old aircraft carrier, *Hermes*, was to be scrapped, and the mini-carrier, *Invincible*, was to be sold to Australia. This left only the mini-carrier, *Illustrious*, whose days were plainly numbered. The number of frigates and destroyers was to be cut from 60 to 42, while dockyard capacity was to be substantially reduced. It was of no benefit to the navy that Nott promised that Britain would honour Labour's commitment to provide an additional 3 per cent of GNP for NATO purposes annually until 1985–6.

Inevitably, this review created an uproar in the naval establishment, and the Navy Minister, Keith Speed, resigned in protest: he was not replaced. In the event, the Royal Navy was saved the necessity of contemplating these cuts, at least temporarily, by Argentina's invasion of the Falkland Islands in 1982.

The Rhodesia issue was settled in 1980 in London as a result of negotiations between all parties to the dispute. The black African majority was given equal voting rights with the white minority and the black anti-Smith guerrillas were to be disarmed under the supervision of British troops. This led to the setting up of a black government in Rhodesia, although the whites retained a few safeguards under the new constitution. The Thatcher government had finally settled one of Britain's few remaining overseas problems, and with the negotiations with the Communist government of China to arrange for the handing over to them of Hong Kong when the lease for the New Territories expired in 1999, it appeared that Britain's overseas commitments were well on their way to liquidation. Moreover, the level of violence in Northern Ireland began to decline after 1980, and the British government was able to replace some of its military units in the Province by the Royal Ulster Constabulary, which had been reorganized in the 1970s. However, the situation remained tense and a new wave of sectarian violence erupted in 1987.

The Falklands War

The Falkland Islands, consisting of East and West Falkland Islands and 100 smaller islands, and the dependencies of South Georgia and the South Sandwich Islands, had been in Britain's possession since the end of the eighteenth century. It had long been Argentina's aspiration to annex these islands on the grounds that they had been seized illegally from Spain by Britain, when they had been part of Spain's Argentinian dominions, and that as the successor to Spain they rightfully belonged to Argentina.

The islanders had a form of internal self-government, based on a Legislative Council with six elected members, but Britain was responsible for defence and foreign policy. Argentina revived her claims in 1965 at the United Nations, and thereafter the Foreign Office entered into negotiations with her to try to find a compromise solution. Its efforts, however, came up against the vociferous opposition of the islanders to any settlement which infringed their rights. Later, Britain proposed the transfer of the sovereignty of the islands to Argentina, with Buenos Aires leasing the islands back to Britain for a number of years, which would enable Britain to continue to defend the interests of the islanders. This plan was also rejected by the islanders.

Argentina began to suspect that the Foreign Office was using the negotiations as a means of putting off a decision about the future of the islands for as long as possible, and when there were rumours of a possible Argentinian descent on the Falklands in 1977 the Callaghan government sent two frigates and a submarine to patrol the seas around the islands. In 1982 Callaghan claimed that this had been sufficient to deter the Argentinians from an invasion, but since the despatch of the vessels was undertaken in considerable secrecy it is difficult to assess the truth of this.

In 1981, as part of the package of naval cuts in Nott's defence budget, the British ice patrol vessel, *Endurance*, was to be withdrawn from the South Atlantic, leaving the islands without any British naval protection. Buenos Aires may well have assumed from this that Britain was not serious about her pledge to defend these possessions. In December 1981, General Leopoldo Galtieri, a member of the junta which ruled Argentina, became President of the country, and it is fairly clear that he looked to the acquisition of the islands as a means of restoring the government's prestige in a country racked by economic and political problems.

British intelligence failed completely to predict Argentina's forthcoming invasion, dismissing increasing rumours and even more reliable information that it was being planned – and much Argentinian newspaper speculation about the subject – as bluff. When some Argentinian scrap metal merchants landed illegally on the island of South Georgia in March, the British government was not disposed to take their antics very seriously, but when they refused to leave, London became concerned and ordered the *Endurance*, which had not yet been withdrawn from service, back to South Georgia. By the end of March the British government was at last aware that Argentina was planning some coup and sent a nuclear submarine to the South Atlantic. It was too late: the Argentinian invasion force had already set sail; and on Friday 2 April her troops had landed on the Falklands and soon overwhelmed the 40 British marines there. South Georgia also fell to the invaders.

President Galtieri assumed that the British would agree to accept the *fait accompli*. However, the British Cabinet had ordered the preparation of a naval task force at Portsmouth on 2 April and, if the government had had any intention of abandoning the Falklands to their fate, it was soon disabused of this by a stormy and prolonged debate in the House of Commons on Saturday 3 April, when the government was bitterly attacked from all sides for its ineptness in not having recognized the threat earlier and for failing as a result to take the necessary defensive measures. The Prime Minister declared that Britain would take all necessary steps to restore the islands to British rule.

The Foreign Secretary, Lord Carrington, insisted on resigning from the Cabinet on the grounds that, as the responsible Minister, he should accept the blame for the débâcle, although the fault lay as much with the Ministry of Defence, whose insistence on cutting Britain's carrier force in 1981 and reluctance to defend the islands properly had encouraged the Galtieri regime to order the invasion. He was replaced as Foreign Secretary by the former Secretary of Defence, Francis Pym. A special Cabinet sub-committee of the Defence and Overseas Policy Committee was set up which became a kind of War Cabinet to supervise the recapture of the islands or the negotiations leading to their restoration to British rule.

This committee consisted of Mrs Thatcher, the chairman, William Whitelaw, the Home Secretary, Francis Pym, John Nott and Cecil Parkinson, the Conservative Party Chairman, and their advisers, Sir Terence Lewin, the Chief of the Defence Staff, Sir Anthony Acland, the new Foreign Office Permanent Under-secretary, Sir Frank Cooper, the Permanent Under-secretary at the Ministry of Defence, and Sir Robert Armstrong of the Cabinet Office. The Commander of the Task Force, Admiral Sir John Fieldhouse, was based at Northwood in North London.

The Royal Navy was superior in size to the Argentinian navy, which consisted of a heavy cruiser, six destroyers and six frigates, which were equipped with Exocet ship-to-ship missiles against which Britain had no effective counter. The Argentinian air force possessed 120 Mirages, Skyhawks and Canberras, while the Argentinian army had stationed 10,000 men on the islands by the end of April.

Fortunately for Britain, the *Invincible* had not yet been handed over to Australia, while the *Hermes* had not yet been scrapped. These two carriers formed the core of the task force, which comprised the assault ships, *Fearless* and *Intrepid*, both of which had been ear-marked for scrapping in 1981 and subsequently reprieved, nine frigates and destroyers, together with support ships of all kinds, many mobilized from civilian companies and including the liners *Canberra* and *QE2*. There were also 22 Sea Harriers and 140 Sea King and Wessex helicopters with the fleet. It set sail for the British-owned Ascension Islands on the first leg of its 50-day voyage to the Falklands on 5 and 6 April: it was joined by a further seven frigates at Gibraltar. There were 44 warships in all, with a total complement of 28,000 men, 10,000 of whom were land forces.

Pym hoped that the knowledge that this task force was on its way would induce the Argentinian government to abandon the islands, and the British government mobilized all its diplomatic resources to ensure that the utmost international pressure was brought to bear on Buenos Aires to yield. Her partners in the European Economic Community, where there was some sympathy for Argentina, particularly in Italy, somewhat grudgingly agreed to impose sanctions on Argentina for a temporary period, but Britain's greatest success was in persuading the United Nations Security Council in Resolution 502 on 3 April to call on Argentina to withdraw its forces immediately from the Falklands and agree to a diplomatic settlement of the dispute. This was passed by a two-thirds majority. Under Article 51 of the United Nations Charter Britain was allowed to take unilateral action to recover the islands if the Argentinians refused to give way.

On 1 May 13 ships of the task force arrived in the territorial waters of the Falkland Islands and the British government imposed a total exclusion zone to all foreign shipping 200 miles around the islands. During April it had become clear that Argentina would not withdraw voluntarily from the islands, despite the efforts at shuttle diplomacy between Buenos Aires and London by Alexander Haig, the American Secretary of State, in an effort to mediate an end to the dispute. The task force therefore prepared to defeat the Argentinian navy, an essential prerequisite for a successful landing. The air defence of the British fleet was the responsibility of the Sea Harriers on board *Hermes* and *Illustrious*, although these planes possessed no radar system which could give their pilots early warning of enemy air or missile attack. The task force did not have many assault landing ships and there were too few helicopters.

The War Cabinet ordered the recapture of the island of South Georgia, which had been the first to fall to the

Argentinians, and on 25 April 1982 this was seized by a detachment of marines, Special Air Service and Special Boat Squadron forces, with no British casualties and one Argentinian sailor killed and the sinking of one Argentinian submarine. The prospects for the success of the invasion were enhanced when, after Galtieri had rejected Haig's last peace proposal, the United States imposed economic sanctions on Argentina on 30 April and began to supply aid to Britain in the form of fuel, ammunition, missiles and signals intelligence.

The first stage in the recapture of the islands was a British air and naval bombardment of the Argentinian base and airport near the capital, Port Stanley, with the British flying Canberra bombers from the Ascension Islands to assist the Sea Harriers in the air attacks. The British lost two Canberras and the Argentinians two Mirages in these attacks. Then, on 2 May, the old Argentinian cruiser, *The General Belgrano*, was sunk by torpedoes fired from the British submarine *Conqueror* with the loss of 368 sailors. This led to considerable outcry in Britain and elsewhere that it had been sunk outside the total exclusion zone and that there was no evidence that it was on course to attack the task force. However, the British commander felt that no risks could be taken that the task force was not the intended victim of the *Belgrano*, and after the sinking the Argentinian navy never ventured out of its mainland ports again during the conflict. On 3 May the Argentinians retaliated by sinking HMS *Sheffield*, a T334 destroyer, with air-launched Sea Dart Exocet missiles. The *Sheffield*'s defences could not hit low-level targets and it was in any case a poorly armoured vessel. Britain lost 21 sailors on the *Sheffield*.

Although the British failed to secure air superiority over the Argentinians, the War Cabinet decided on 8 May that the assault on the islands should now go ahead: the Special Air Service had already landed to reconnoitre enemy defences. British commandos established beach heads on both sides of Port San Carlos Bay on 21 May and the landing forces were soon on their way towards the twin objectives of Port Stanley and Goose Green. In the battle for San Carlos Bay the British found themselves facing sustained Argentinian air attack and they lost two frigates, a destroyer, a landing ship and a container ship. However, on 29 May Goose Green was recaptured from the Argentinians, while on 8 June British reinforcements were landed at Bluff Cove. Finally, on Monday 14 June General M. Menendez, the Commander of the Argentinian forces on the Falklands, surrendered all his forces on the islands and 11,313 Argentinian prisoners fell into British hands and were repatriated to the mainland.

This was a signal success for Britain's armed forces, and the expedition with which the task force was assembled and despatched contrasted with the slow and cumbersome nature of the preparations for the Suez campaign in 1956. Nevertheless, as with so many previous British expeditions of this kind, it was hastily planned while the intelligence available to the British was poor. Fortunately, these did not affect the outcome. While the Argentinian conscripts suffered from poor leadership and an inadequate diet, they considerably outnumbered the British invaders, while the quality of their air force was excellent: a few more successful Exocet firings and the British task force would have been in a parlous position. But the British had taken a successful gamble which redounded to their prestige internationally and led to a considerable increase in the popularity of Mrs Thatcher's government at home. This was probably the last of Britain's colonial wars, with Britain losing 225 men killed and 777 wounded (she had deployed 28,000 men), six ships sunk and ten damaged, and nine Harriers lost out of an initial complement of 26. The government estimated the costs of the expedition at £700 million, with a further £800 million to cover the losses she had sustained. The Argentinians lost 652 men during the conflict.

Defence policy after the Falklands War

Some lessons were learned from Britain's experiences during this conflict. There were some improvements, for instance, made to ship defences in the light of the sinking of HMS *Sheffield*. The long-term influence on British defence policy of this conflict is, however, less clear. The cost of improving the defences of the Falkland Islands, over which the Thatcher government is committed to retain British sovereignty, will be fairly high, at least in the short run: some £250 million altogether.

Between 1979 and 1985 defence expenditure rose by 18 per cent in real terms, with 46 per cent of the defence budget spent on equipment. This is a higher figure than that spent on defence by any other European NATO power. The Armed Forces Pay Review Body recommended a rise of 7.5 per cent for the 1986–7 financial year, although the government would only agree to its being paid from 1 July rather than from 1 April 1986. With the end of the 3 per cent extra per annum expenditure on NATO forces in 1986, the government promised level funding of defence for the rest of the decade. George Younger, who replaced Michael Heseltine as Defence Secretary in 1986, told the House of Commons Defence Committee that he did not believe that Britain would have 'to withdraw from any major commitment or major part thereof' for the next few years.

The *Statement on the Defence Estimates* of 1987 did not mention any drastic cuts in expenditure but extolled the importance of Britain's contribution to NATO which, it claimed, represented 95 per cent of Britain's defence budget.[5] It defined the main roles for Britain in NATO as:

the provision of nuclear forces, including the maintenance of an independent nuclear deterrent;
defence of the United Kingdom itself, our homeland and a vital support base for NATO;
land and air forces based in Europe and contributing to forward defence, together with the capability for massive reinforcement from the United Kingdom, if required; and
maritime forces in the Eastern Atlantic and Channel areas, and contributing to forward defence in the Norwegian Sea.

This statement also repeated the theme of previous statements about the importance of 'the partnership of the Old World and the New', and of the crucial contribution 'to collective security by the presence of substantial US and Canadian forces in Europe'. There was therefore little indication in 1987 that the government was contemplating any major reduction in defence expenditure, assuming perhaps that the ending of the additional 3 per cent commitment to NATO in 1986 was sufficient reduction for the time being. However, the size of the Royal Navy continued to fall, albeit in manpower rather than ships: between 1985 and 1986 it fell to 60,262 personnel (a 4 per cent cut) and it was to fall by a further 1,100 by 1 April 1987. The government is, however, committed to maintaining a force of destroyers and frigates of about 50 ships, and it is difficult to see how further savings can be made in the Royal Navy vote if this is to be adhered to. Moreover, attacks on neutral shipping in the Persian Gulf by the Iranians forced the British government to send destroyers and minesweepers into Gulf waters to protect British shipping in 1987.

The government's White Paper on Public Spending in January 1988 gave the following figures for past and future defence expenditure at 1986–7 prices:

1982–3	1983–4	1984–5	1985–6	1986–7	1988–9	1989–90	1990–1
17,135	17,647	18,744	18,495	18,149	17,631	17,700	17,700

This suggested that expenditure on defence would fall by 2.5 per cent between 1987–8 and 1988–9. This fall will create serious problems for George Younger, who will have to decide whether his pledge to maintain existing commitments will be honoured or whether he will have to withdraw from some of the expensive collaborative European projects for the 1990s into which Britain has entered with her European NATO allies: a third generation anti-tank guided weapon system, in which eight NATO nations are to participate, a new NATO frigate, a new helicopter (the EH01), in collaboration with Italy, using the British experimental rotor system (BERP), which makes it possible to achieve greater speeds than ever before, and a European fighter aircraft. On the other hand, the recent Soviet–American agreement to remove all intermediate nuclear forces from Europe will inevitably lead to pressures on the West for further reductions in expenditure.

Conclusion

Britain now devotes 95 per cent of her defence expenditure to the NATO area. She maintains an army of 55,000 in the NATO Central Region (Western Germany) and has promised to increase this to 56,000 by 1999. This consists of four armoured divisions plus an artillery division, together with 13 air squadrons in RAF Germany. A further 150,000 troops would be despatched to Western Europe after mobilization. She has also expanded the size of the Territorial Army to six infantry battalions since 1986.

The RAF is now composed of three Commands: Strike (formed in 1967 from the former Fighter and Bomber Commands), Support (training and back-up forces) and RAF Germany, with Tornado and Jaguar strike aircraft. With her naval and air elements, Britain contributes to all three of NATO's missions: strategic nuclear, tactical nuclear and conventional. Whether these 'balanced forces' can be sustained in the long run depends on economic factors and whether politicians and public opinion continue to accept that the effort is worth while. The present government is committed to maintain the armed services and the nuclear deterrent at their existing levels, but it is a matter of conjecture as to whether a future government will regard itself as similarly committed.

Notes

1 *Defence: Open Government Document 81/2* (London, HMSO, March 1982).
2 Quoted in Phil Williams, 'Meeting alliance and national needs', in John Roper (ed.) *The Future of British Defence Policy* (London, 1985), p. 17.
3 *The United Kingdom Defence Programme: the Way Forward* (London, HMSO, Cmnd 8288, June 1981). See Appendix V.
4 House of Commons, *Second Report of the Defence Estimates Committee* (London, HMSO, 5 June 1986), p. vi.
5 *Statement on the Defence Estimates* (London, HMSO, Cmnd 101-1, 1987).

9 Conclusion

There are two main schools of thought amongst British academics about how British defence policy has developed since 1945. The first, which has been put forward by John Baylis, M. Chichester and J. Wilkinson argues that 'the ideology of decline permeates much of the existing literature on defence and acts as a kind of "paradigm" within which much of the academic discourse takes place.'[1] This has been described as the 'orthodox' view which attributes the reduction in the size of Britain's defence establishment since 1945 entirely to financial and economic pressures which forced successive British governments into making hasty and piecemeal cuts.[2]

The other school of thought is represented by David Greenwood, who believes that the 'orthodox' version does not provide a satisfactory explanation for the immense changes that have taken place since the end of the Second World War. He sees the process not as a haphazard one, as merely a reaction to economic difficulties, but as a continuous adjustment to new circumstances and conditions. In this view, Britain's defence policy-making has been based on more rational considerations than Baylis and company are prepared to concede. As a result, Britain's defences have been frequently reshaped and restructured since 1945 in order to meet the immediate needs of her security.[3]

One must agree that to ascribe decline to a situation where Britain has maintained a fairly consistent average annual expenditure on defence of about 5–6 per cent of GNP since

1945, a much higher percentage than that spent by her European NATO allies, and which has enabled her in 1988 to occupy the fourth or fifth position in the global military league, is rather excessive. A more satisfactory explanation might be that, over a long period of time, Britain came to recognize that the bulk of her overseas commitments, which required the maintenance of a large military organization, had become irrelevant to her vital interests as a result of her progressive abandonment of Empire between 1947 and the early 1960s. Furthermore, they were also a drain on her faltering economy. Very few of the major decisions on defence issues which British governments made in this period were a panic reaction in the face of major crises and none was taken without much heart-searching and careful consideration of the possible options.

The Labour Party had long been committed to granting independence to India before 1945: it was the timing that remained in doubt, almost to the last moment. While the process of independence inflicted enormous suffering on the Hindu and Moslem populations of the sub-continent, the last British troops left Bombay in 1948 without having had to undergo the bitter experiences of the French in Indo-China and Algeria or the Dutch in Indonesia. The Macmillan government's policy of decolonization after 1957 was based on the similar calculation that Britain could not withstand the wave of nationalist agitation that was spreading across Africa without suffering heavy and unnecessary casualties: that the cost of remaining would be out of proportion to the advantages that might accrue. A voluntary and early withdrawal was seen as the best way of achieving a peaceful and relatively smooth transfer of power to moderate nationalist forces, however unsatisfactory the subsequent outcome may have been in many cases.

The belated decision by the Wilson government in 1968 to abandon Britain's pretensions east of Suez was the one clear case where the pressure of economic circumstances forced Britain into a sudden change of course which in the short run caused great irritation and inconvenience to Britain's friends and allies in the Far East. No doubt, the British government should have concluded much earlier that Britain's role east of Suez was redundant and made more careful preparations in advance to ease the effects of her evacuation of the region. However, before 1968 the maintenance of these extra-European commitments was still seen as essential in order to defend Britain's interests, while Harold Wilson was also convinced that Britain's presence east of Suez had an importance which transcended purely material considerations.

Nor was the Sandys White Paper of 1957 by any means a sudden improvisation. It was the product of a long debate in the British defence policy-making establishment, an influential section of which argued that Britain's possession of nuclear weapons would enable her to make sweeping reductions in the size of her conventional military forces. The Suez débâcle and the ensuing financial crisis finally convinced a much wider circle of politicians and military leaders that drastic steps had to be taken immediately to cut Britain's escalating military expenditure, and the only way to achieve this was by relying in future on nuclear deterrence. The exercise turned out to be self-defeating in the long run since Sandys did not propose that Britain make any major reductions in her overseas commitments which were the root cause of her heavy financial burdens, while the 'independent' deterrent proved to be more expensive than had been anticipated. Britain's nuclear weapons were irrelevant to the task of protecting the internal security of her remaining overseas possessions. The White Paper was not the revolutionary document that it was proclaimed to be at the time.

The decline in the size of Britain's armed forces since the late 1940s can therefore be seen as the result of a continuous process of adaptation to a world whose configuration has changed out of all recognition over the past four decades. In this context, therefore, Britain's reduction in status from a great power to a regional power, and the loss of much of the world-wide influence she possessed before 1960, was the result of new international circumstances and had little to do with the size of her military establishment. She did not find that her global role between 1960 and 1968 gave her much influence over American policies. The large and cumbersome forces Britain maintained across the globe in 1950 would be totally inappropriate to the requirements of British security in the

1980s which require a high standard of professional expertise and technical skills. Apart from her action over the Falkland Islands in 1982 and her recent excursion into the Persian Gulf, Britain's defence efforts are today concentrated entirely on Western Europe, and her armed forces have been restructured to take account of this. Greenwood argues that in fact the quality of Britain's army, navy and air force is far superior to anything she has been able to achieve in the past and that as a result her effective military power is far stronger.[4] In any case, economic success now seems to be rated higher than military might as an indicator of the strength of a nation – as Japan demonstrates – although of course this is not to deny the continuing importance of the ability to project military power.

The withdrawal of Britain from her overseas responsibilities and the consequent diminution in the size of her armed services was not, of course, accomplished without considerable strains and tensions both within Britain's armed services and in the country at large. Internal costs have been high, since a large segment of British industry is dependent on orders for ships, airplanes and military equipment of all kinds for its continued survival. For instance, in 1946 Britain possessed 23 major airframe manufacturers and nine major aeroengine companies. By 1974, successive cut-backs had taken their toll: mergers and bankruptcies had reduced this number to six airframe and one aeroengine manufacturer, Rolls Royce. The latter was now dependent on government subsidies. In 1977, three of the airframe companies were nationalized and amalgamated, while a fourth, Short Brothers,[5] was 98 per cent state-owned, and a fifth, Westland, which produced helicopters, was the subject of a bitter row between the Department of Defence and the Department of Trade and Industry in 1984 which led to the resignation of both Secretaries of State.

Since Defence Ministry orders account for 400,000 jobs in the economy, the viability of the defence industries is a matter of continuing concern, and inevitably closures or take-overs by foreign companies have occasioned furious debate, although in the case of Westland the dispute involved the question of its absorption by an American multinational or its rescue by a consortium of European companies. Defence production is a risky business for all concerned. It can take up to 12 years to procure a modern aircraft or tank from the design stage to the manufacture of the finished product, involving about 400 designers and technicians and countless managerial and shop-floor workers. Under these circumstances, costly mistakes were inevitable as governments found themselves faced with the problem of whether to persist with or cancel systems which had been authorized by their predecessors and whose future viability had become problematic. By 1967, 32 weapons systems had been cancelled, playing havoc with the defence industries affected and creating large-scale unemployment in the cities where those industries were located.

Whether or not there will be further retraction in Britain's defence industries will, of course, depend on decisions made in Whitehall about Britain's future defence policy. Another round of financial retrenchment or greater dependence on arms purchases from the United States will lead to further closures and amalgamations. Since the 1970s, the Department of Defence has tried to provide Britain's defence industries with a broader base by a drive to increase Britain's arms export trade, particularly to the Middle East. But this effort can be full of pitfalls, as in the case of Iran, where the revolutionary government which toppled the Shah repudiated an agreement to buy 1,200 British Chieftain tanks signed by the Shah's government, plunging Britain's tank industry into acute financial difficulties.

Britain has continued to demonstrate a skill in perfecting new military techniques, such as the development of Chobham armour and her advances in helicopter design. For the future, her ability to keep abreast in such areas as new precision-guided weapons, using laser and thermal guidance techniques for anti-tank, anti-aircraft and anti-ship warfare, will be of crucial importance for her survival as a second-rank power.

It is clear that Britain will remain a nuclear power into the 1990s with Trident replacing Polaris as her only strategic delivery system. Of course, developments in anti-submarine warfare or Soviet advances in strategic defences might render Trident vulnerable to interdiction and therefore useless as a deterrent. However, the long-standing British fear that her deterrent might be negotiated away as a result of bilateral strategic arms negotiations between the United States and the Soviet Union were assuaged to some extent by the acceptance by the Soviet leader, Mikhail Gorbachev, at the Reykjavik summit meeting in October 1986, of President Reagan's insistence that the Anglo-French nuclear forces would not be the subject of negotiations at the Geneva strategic arms talks.

There have been four major defence reviews since 1950. If the British government concludes that a further round of defence cuts is necessary, there might soon be a fifth. What form this will take is uncertain. Lawrence Freedman has suggested that:

> the options would appear to be the extraction of extra funds from the Treasury, a full-scale defence review, or (most likely) what has come to be called a defence review by stealth – or perhaps more accurately, a defence review by drift. The latter is politically the least controversial. It involves managing the defence budget in such a way that no fundamental decisions are taken with regard to roles and commitment, and ways are sought to find savings within the established framework.[6]

If Freedman is correct in this assumption, the situation will be similar to that which pertained between 1960 and 1968, where major decisions were avoided and reductions were made within the existing structure. One fears, however, that the end result will be similar to that which occurred in 1968, this time with a sudden and ill thought-out abandonment of one of Britain's major commitments to NATO, causing the utmost confusion and anger to all concerned.

Notes

1 Quoted in Tony McGrew, 'British defence policy: decline or transformation?', paper presented to the BISA Conference in 1987 at the University College of Wales, Aberystwyth, p. 2.
2 John Baylis, '"Greenwoodery" and British defence policy', *International Affairs*, vol. 62, no. 3 (summer 1986), pp. 443–57.
3 McGrew, 'British defence policy', p. 7.

4 David Greenwood, 'Defence and national priorities since 1945', in John Baylis (ed.), *British Defence Policy in a Changing World* (London, 1977), p. 189.
5 Dan Smith, *The Defence of the Realm in the 1980s* (London, 1980).
6 Lawrence Freedman, 'The strategic concept', in Philip Sabin (ed.), *The Future of United Kingdom Air Power* (London, 1988).

Appendix I
Future Defence Policy: Report by the Chiefs of Staff, 22 May 1947

Part I Commonwealth defence policy

3   The United Kingdom, as the senior member of the British Commonwealth and a Great Power, must be prepared at all times to fulfil her responsibilities not only to the United Nations but also to herself as a Great Power. To fulfil her obligations, she must achieve a strong and sound economy which will give her the ability to expand industry and the armed forces immediately on to a war basis....

Possible Threats to World Peace

7   Although we do not regard a future war as inevitable, we cannot yet be sure that all the Great Powers are determined to keep the peace. Until the general political atmosphere improves, we cannot, therefore, rule out the possibility of war with Russia, either by actual aggression on her part or by a miscalculation of the extent to which she can pursue a policy of ideological and territorial expansion short of war with the Democratic Powers.

8   The issue which cannot be avoided is that our Defence Policy must at present be based on the possibility of war with Russia. We do not consider that Germany by herself will constitute a danger for many years, but should a resurgent Germany again become a menace, it would be possible to adjust our Defence Policy, if we have meanwhile prepared against a presently greater threat.

© Crown copyright. Extracts reproduced by permission of the Controller of Her Majesty's Stationery Office. DESE 5/4. Reproduced in Julian Lewis, *Changing Direction: British Military Planning for Post-war Strategic Defence 1942–1947* (London, 1988), pp. 370–87.

9   We are convinced that we can reduce the risk of war if from now onwards we and our potential allies show strength and a preparedness to use this strength if necessary....

European Allies

12   In the past we have relied on building up an alliance of European countries to unite with us from the very beginning in resisting aggression. There is now, however, no combination of European Powers capable of standing up to Russia on land, nor do we think that the probable military capabilities of an association of European States at present justify us in relying upon such an association for our defence.

Nevertheless, any time which we can gain to improve our defences would be of such value that every effort should be made to organise an association of Western European Powers, which would at least delay the enemy's advance across Europe....

Support from the United States

13   We must have the active and very early support of the United States. The United States alone, because of her man-power, industrial resources and her lead in the development of weapons of mass destruction, can turn the balance in favour of the Democracies. Apart from other considerations the United States will for some years at any rate, be the sole source from which we can draw a supply of atomic bombs....

Middle East

15   The area in which Russian expansion would be easiest and at the same time would hurt us most would be the Middle East. We may be sure that if we abandon our position there in peace Russia will fill the vacuum.

16   The importance of the Middle East as a centre of Commonwealth communications remains, and will remain, beyond question....

Implications of New Weapons

22   The main implications of the new weapons likely to be available by the critical period about 1956 may be summarised as follows:

(a) The possibility exists of achieving rapid and decisive results by the use of mass destruction weapons against economic key targets and the civil population.

(b) Owing to the vastly greater destructive power of atomic and biological weapons, acceptable standards of defence have gone up immeasurably. Within the next ten years there is little possibility that these higher standards of defence can be reached.

(c) There are greater possibilities than before of surprise attack, since the preparations required to deliver decisive attacks with the new weapons could be on a smaller scale than with conventional weapons. Militarily we must be prepared to exploit any such opportunity, although politically we are always likely to be severely handicapped.

(d) The potential threat to our sea communications will be greater than at any time in the last war. . . .

Fundamentals of our defence policy

33 From all the above factors we can now deduce the fundamentals of our Defence Policy:

(a) The supreme object of British policy is to prevent war, provided that this can be done without prejudicing our vital interests. This entails support of the United Nations and ability to defend our own interests.

(b) The most likely and most formidable threat to our interests comes from Russia, especially from 1956 onwards, and it is against this worst case that we must be prepared, at the same time taking every possible step to prevent it.

(c) The most effective step towards preventing war is tangible evidence that we possess adequate forces and resources, that we are fully prepared and that we have the intention and ability to take immediate offensive action.

(d) Essential measures required in peace to give us a chance of survival and victory in the event of war are:
   (i) Retaining at a high state of readiness properly balanced armed forces for immediate use on the outbreak of war, with the necessary reserves of resources to support them.
   (ii) Maintaining the united front of the British Commonwealth and doing everything possible to ensure that in the

event of war we have the immediate and active support of all its members.
(iii) Ensuring that we have the active and early support of the United States of America and of the Western European States.
(iv) Increasing and exploiting our present scientific and technical lead, especially in the development of weapons of mass destruction.
(v) Actively opposing the spread of Russian influence by adopting a firm attitude to further Russian territorial and ideological expansion, particularly in all areas of strategic value to the defence of the British Commonwealth.
(vi) Arresting by all possible means the deterioration that has already begun in our own position and prestige in the Middle East, and encouraging the continued independence of Greece and Turkey.
(vii) Maintaining our Intelligence Organisations at a high standard of efficiency.
(viii) Being prepared to take offensive air action from the outset since the war will rapidly reach a climax and the endurance of the United Kingdom cannot be guaranteed for any considerable period against attacks by modern weapons, still less by weapons of mass destruction. The best bases for this offensive action are United Kingdom, Middle East and if possible North-West India.
(ix) Being ourselves prepared, equipped and able to use weapons of mass destruction as a part of this offensive action. . . .

Part II   The strategy of Commonwealth defence

Basic requirements of our strategy

36   It is now apparent that in pursuance of our Defence Policy the following are the basic requirements of our strategy:
   (a) The defence of the United Kingdom and its development as an offensive base.
   (b) The control of essential sea communications.
   (c) A firm hold in the Middle East and its development as an offensive base.

These three pillars of our strategy must stand together. The collapse of any one of them will bring down the whole structure of Commonwealth Strategy.

To them we would add a fourth, which though not essential would give a most desirable addition of strength:

(d) The co-operation of India: the provision of the necessary assistance to ensure her security; and the development of an offensive base in North-West India....

Conclusion – tasks of the armed forces and principles affecting their build-up

47 Our strategic needs lead to conclusions on the tasks of our Armed Forces which can now be stated in general terms. It is also possible to indicate certain general principles which should govern the nature and size of our future forces:

(a) *Research and development* Our first requirement is to build up our organisation for scientific research and development to a level which will ensure that we can maintain our technical superiority on the one hand, and on the other provide the necessary information to enable us to decide in good time on our re-equipment policy.

(b) *Offensive force* As our ability to strike will represent both a very strong deterrent to aggression and one of our principal means of defence, the development of an air offensive force must be given high priority.

(c) *Defence of the United Kingdom* The security of the United Kingdom is of vital importance. While the possession of a powerful offensive force is essential to our security, the development of our active and passive air defence organisations, in all their aspects, must be complementary to the build-up of our air striking force.

The Army must provide for the manning of the anti-aircraft defences; readiness to aid the Civil Power, and defence against invasion, primarily by air.

The Navy and the RAF must ensure control over the waters surrounding these islands.

(d) *Control of sea communications* While our ability to hit back and the knowledge that we possess a sound defence will be a very strong deterrent to a potential aggressor, once war starts the security of our sea communications will rapidly assume vital importance.

The task of the Navy, assisted by the RAF, will be to secure to our own use sea communications, not only in the approaches to the United Kingdom but world-wide with the Dominions, the United States and sources of supply, and also through the Mediterranean to the Middle East; at the same time denying them to the enemy.

The maintenance and development in peace of the necessary naval and air forces to ensure security and control against any threat or challenge will therefore continue to be of high importance.

At present it appears that the chief threats to our sea communications will be from fast submarine attack, air attack and minelaying. But the threat of surface attacks on our shipping must still be guarded against and the capacity of the potential enemy to challenge our control of sea communications must be constantly watched and provided against.

(e) *Defence of the Middle East and India* The primary task of the Army, apart from the manning of anti-aircraft defences and readiness to aid civil power in the United Kingdom, will be to ensure the security of our Middle East base. Despite the possible risk of invasion of the United Kingdom by air we consider the provision of forces to meet our requirements in the Middle East must be given priority over the anti-invasion role in the United Kingdom.

Air forces will be required for the defence of the Middle East base and in support of the Army there. They will also be required in India if she is co-operating with us.

Naval forces capable of giving all necessary support to the Army's land battle will be required.

(f) *Combined operations* We do not foresee a necessity for major combined operations, in the form of assault landings by sea or air, in the early stages of a war. Nor would our military strength at the outset permit of their being undertaken. But it is impossible to forecast how the war would develop. Minor landings in furtherance of a land campaign already undertaken might be required. When the full strength of the Commonwealth and the Allies is built up, and an overseas operation is necessary, combined operations on a large scale may be required.

It will, therefore, be necessary in peace to provide for keeping the art of Combined Operations and Airborne Assault alive in all the Armed Forces, and for research, experiment and development in the technique required.

(Signed)

J. H. D. CUNNINGHAM
MONTGOMERY of ALAMEIN
W. F. DICKSON (V.C.A.S.)

Appendix II
Defence: Outline of Future Policy, 1957

Need for New Approach

As previous Statements on Defence have emphasised, Britain's defence policy is determined by her obligation to make her contribution to NATO and other alliances for collective defence, as well as to discharge her own special responsibilities in many parts of the world.

2   The present shape of Britain's defence forces was largely settled by the rearmament programme launched in 1950 at the time of the Korean War. However, the ending of hostilities in Korea radically altered the position. The immediate danger of major war receded and was replaced by the prospect of a prolonged period of acute international tension. It was clear that the plan for a short intensive rearmament spurt no longer fitted the needs of the situation, and that for it must be substituted the conception of the 'long haul'. It also became evident that a military effort on the scale planned in 1950, which envisaged expenditure amounting to £4,700 million over three years, was beyond the country's capacity. In an endeavour to keep the cost within bounds, the programme was slowed down and spread out over a longer period.

3   However, the time has now come to revise not merely the size, but the whole character of the defence plan. The Communist threat remains, but its nature has changed; and it is now evident that, on both military and economic grounds, it is necessary to make a fresh appreciation of the problem and to adopt a new approach towards it.

London, HMSO, Cmd 124. Reproduced by kind permission of the Controller of HM Stationery Office.

Scientific Advances

4 In recent years military technology has been making dramatic strides. New and ever more formidable weapons have been succeeding one another at an increasing rate. In less than a decade, the atom bomb dropped at Hiroshima has been overtaken by the far more powerful hydrogen or megaton bomb. Parallel with this, the evolution of rocket weapons of all kinds, both offensive and defensive, has been proceeding apace.

5 It has been clear for some time that these scientific advances must fundamentally alter the whole basis of military planning....

Demands on Economic Resources

7 Over the last five years, defence has on average absorbed 10 per cent of Britain's gross national product. Some 7 per cent of the working population are either in the Services or supporting them. One-eighth of the output of the metal-using industries, upon which the export trade so largely depends, is devoted to defence. An undue proportion of qualified scientists and engineers are engaged on military work. In addition, the retention of such large forces abroad gives rise to heavy charges which place a severe strain upon the balance of payments....

Collective Defence

10 The growth in the power of weapons of mass destruction has emphasised the fact that no country can any longer protect itself in isolation. The defence of Britain is possible only as part of the collective defence of the free world. This conception of collective defence is the basis of the North Atlantic, South-East Asia and Baghdad alliances....

Nuclear Deterrent

12 It must be frankly recognised that there is at present no means of providing adequate protection for the people of this country against the consequences of an attack with nuclear weapons. Though, in the event of war, the fighter aircraft of the Royal Air Force would unquestionably be able to take a heavy toll of enemy bombers, a proportion would inevitably get through. Even if it were only a dozen, they could with megaton bombs inflict widespread devastation....

Appendix II 141

15   The free world is to-day mainly dependent for its protection upon the nuclear capacity of the United States. While Britain cannot by comparison make more than a modest contribution, there is a wide measure of agreement that she must possess an appreciable element of nuclear deterrent power of her own. British atomic bombs are already in steady production and the Royal Air Force holds a substantial number of them. A British megaton weapon has now been developed. This will shortly be tested and thereafter a stock will be manufactured.

16   The means of delivering these weapons is provided at present by medium bombers of the V-class, whose performance in speed and altitude is comparable to that of any bomber aircraft now in service in any other country. It is the intention that these should be supplemented by ballistic rockets. Agreement in principle has recently been reached with the United States Government for the supply of some medium-range missiles of this type. . . .

Europe and Atlantic

20   The possession of nuclear air power is not by itself a complete deterrent. The frontiers of the free world, particularly in Europe, must be firmly defended on the ground. For only in this way can it be made clear that aggression will be resisted.

21   Britain must provide her fair share of the armed forces needed for this purpose. However, she cannot any longer continue to make a disproportionately large contribution.

22   Accordingly, Her Majesty's Government, after consultation with the Allied Governments in the North Atlantic Council and in the Council of the Western European Union, have felt it necessary to make reductions in the British land and air forces on the Continent. The strength of the British Army of the Rhine will be reduced from about 77,000 to about 64,000 during the next twelve months; and, subject to consultation with the Allied Governments in the autumn, further reductions will be made thereafter. The force will be re-organised in such a way as to increase the proportion of fighting units; and atomic rocket artillery will be introduced which will greatly augment their fire-power.

23   The aircraft of the Second Tactical Air Force in Germany will be reduced to about half their present number by the end of March, 1958. This reduction will be offset by the fact that some of the squadrons will be provided with atomic bombs. A similar reduction

will be made in the light bomber force in England, which is assigned to NATO. . . .

Middle East

25   Outside the area covered by the North Atlantic Alliance, Britain has military responsibilities in other parts of the world, in particular in the Middle East and South-East Asia.

26   Apart from its own importance, the Middle East guards the right flank of NATO and is the gateway to the African continent. In the Arabian Peninsula, Britain must at all times be ready to defend Aden Colony and Protectorates and the territories on the Persian Gulf for whose defence she is responsible. For this task, land, air and sea forces have to be maintained in that area and in East Africa.

27   In addition, Britain has undertaken in the Baghdad Pact to co-operate with the other signatory States for security and defence, and for the prevention of Communist encroachment and infiltration. In the event of emergency, British forces in the Middle East area would be made available to support the Alliance. These would include bomber squadrons based in Cyprus capable of delivering nuclear weapons.

28   As a result of the termination of the treaty with Jordan, Britain has been relieved of the responsibility for defending that country in the event of attack; and British forces are being withdrawn. The British troops in Libya will also be progressively reduced.

Far East

29   In South-East Asia, apart from defending her colonies and protectorates, Britain has agreed to assist in the external defence of Malaya after she attains independence. Britain also has an international commitment, as a member of the SEATO and ANZAM defence systems, to help preserve stability and resist the extension of Communist power in that area.

30   It is proposed to maintain in this theatre a mixed British–Gurkha force and certain air force elements, together with a substantial garrison in Hong Kong and a small naval force based on Singapore.

31   In addition, there is a Commonwealth Strategic Reserve. This includes a brigade to which Britain contributes two battalions.

Australia and New Zealand jointly provide the remainder of the brigade and some naval and air forces.

32 After consultation with the United States and with the other Commonwealth countries concerned, the Government have decided to withdraw the remaining United Kingdom troops, approximately a battalion, from Korea.

Overseas Garrisons

33 Garrisons for British colonies and protectorates make substantial demands upon military manpower. In view of the increasing strength and efficiency of Colonial forces and the growing capacity to send reinforcements rapidly from Britain, the Government propose to make considerable reductions in these garrisons wherever practicable.

Central Reserve

34 With the reduction in size of garrisons and other British forces overseas, it is more than ever essential to be able to despatch reinforcements at short notice. With this object, a Central Reserve will be maintained in the British Isles....

Sea Power

39 It is the Government's intention to maintain British naval strength East of Suez at about its present level. One carrier group will normally be stationed in the Indian Ocean.

Manpower Requirements

40 Provided that the Services are reshaped and redistributed on the lines indicated above and that commitments are curtailed in the manner proposed, the Government are satisfied that Britain could discharge her overseas responsibilities and make an effective contribution to the defence of the free world with armed forces much smaller than at present....

43 National Service inevitably involves an uneconomic use of manpower, especially in the training organisation. There are at present no less than 150,000 men training or being trained in the establishments of the three Services. This high figure is due, in large measure, to the continuous turnover inseparable from National

Service, the abolition of which would make possible substantial savings in manpower. . . .

46 In the light of the need to maintain a balanced distribution of the national resources, the Government have made a comprehensive review of the demands of defence upon the economy and of the country's military responsibilities. They have concluded that it would be right to aim at stabilising the armed forces on an all-regular footing at a strength of about 375,000 by the end of 1962. This does not take account of Colonial troops and other forces enlisted overseas, which at present amount to about 60,000.

National Service

47 The Government have accordingly decided to plan on the basis that there will be no further call-up under the National Service Acts after the end of 1960.

48 It must nevertheless be understood that, if voluntary recruiting fails to produce the numbers required, the country will have to face the need for some limited form of compulsory service to bridge the gap.

49 While the regular element is building up and the total strength of the forces is being run down, the size of the National Service intake will have to be progressively reduced. The result will be that the number of men becoming available for National Service will, to a growing extent, exceed requirements. The Government have prepared plans to effect the call-up of the reduced numbers needed and will shortly announce these to Parliament. . . .

Research and Development

59 A central feature of the defence plan is the maintenance of an effective deterrent. High priority will therefore continue to be given to the development of British nuclear weapons suitable for delivery by manned bombers and ballistic rockets. Nuclear warheads are also being evolved for defensive guided missiles. . . .

Expenditure

70 The Defence Estimates for the year 1956/7 amounted to about £1,600 million, before deducting receipts from Germany and the

United States. Had the programme as planned a year ago been allowed to continue unchanged, the figure for 1957/8 would have risen to about £1,700 million.

71 However, as a result of strenuous efforts to effect economy, it has been found possible to keep the defence estimates for the coming year down to a total of £1,483 million. From this must be deducted receipts from Germany and the United States, which are expected to be about £50 million and £13 million respectively. Thus the net estimate of total defence expenditure for the year 1957/8 will amount to about £1,420 million.

Appendix III
Supplementary Statement on Defence Policy, 1967

I Introduction

2 We announced in Part I of the Statement on the Defence Estimates 1966 (Cmnd 2901) the decisions which we had taken in order to carry us close to the financial objective for 1969–70. Since then, as part of our continuous review of defence policy and programmes, we have looked beyond 1969–70 to determine how much money and how many men we must plan to have in the 1970s both in relation to the commitments which we foresee and to the resources which the country can afford for defence. We have followed the broad approach to future defence policy described in the Defence Review.

3 But we have also taken account of major developments in the last twelve months: political – the evolution of Government policy towards Europe, progress in revising NATO strategy, the Middle East crisis, and changes in South East Asia following the end of 'confrontation'; and economic – a more pressing need to reduce overseas expenditure, a slower rate of growth than expected in the British economy, and the consequent necessity to keep Government expenditure as low as possible.

II Europe

1 The security of Britain still depends above all on the prevention of war in Europe. We, therefore, regard it as essential to maintain both

London, HMSO, July 1967, Cmnd 3357. Reproduced by kind permission of the Controller of HM Stationery Office.

the military efficiency and the political solidarity of the North Atlantic Treaty Organisation. For this purpose, we must continue to make a substantial contribution to NATO's forces in order to play our part in the defence of Europe and to maintain the necessary balance within the Western alliance. This contribution will become even more important as we develop closer political and economic ties between Britain and her European neighbours. . . .

3   Since the publication of the Statement on the Defence Estimates 1967 (Cmnd 3203) last February, NATO has taken an important step in relating its strategy to the political and economic realities of the late 1960s. At their meeting in May 1967, the Defence Ministers of the alliance agreed on the political guidance to be given to the military authorities for future force planning; it was based on a reassessment of the threat confronting the alliance and of the resources available to meet it. . . .

III   Outside Europe

1   The aim of our policy outside Europe is, as we said in the Statement on the Defence Estimates 1967 (Cmnd 3203), 'to foster developments which will enable the local peoples to live at peace without the presence of external forces', and thus to allow our forces to withdraw from their stations in the Middle East and Far East. We cannot predict exactly when the situation will make this possible in every area where our forces are now stationed; and, in planning their withdrawal, we must take account of the impact of our plans on the peoples concerned, and on the policies of our allies. We remain responsible for the security of our dependencies; we have obligations to our friends and allies; and we have a political and economic interest in the stability of the world outside Europe, which makes it desirable to retain a capacity for contributing to the maintenance of peace where we can usefully do so. . . .

5   We have already announced, and gone some way to implement, plans to reduce forces in the Mediterranean, the South Atlantic and the Caribbean. We have also declared our intention to withdraw from South Arabia and the Aden base in January 1968.

6   In the Far East, we have decided to reach a reduction of about half the forces deployed in Singapore and Malaysia during 1970–1.

7 We shall continue to honour our obligations under SEATO, but the forces assigned to specific SEATO plans will be progressively altered in nature and size....

IV The Forces

The Royal Navy

2 The Polaris force will be Britain's contribution to the strategic nuclear deterrent of the West. The Navy will also continue to play a leading part in the maritime shield forces of NATO and will be able to perform, for as far ahead as can be foreseen, a valuable peacekeeping function outside Europe by the unobtrusive and flexible exercise of maritime power. For these roles our naval forces must be able to fight and survive in the environment of the guided-missile and nuclear-powered submarine; they must, therefore, include some ships of the highest capability.

3 Air power will be as indispensable to the Fleet of tomorrow as it is today. HMS *Ark Royal* and HMS *Eagle* will continue in service until the middle 1970s: we plan to phase out HMS *Victorious* and HMS *Hermes* in 1969 and 1971 respectively. After the last carriers go, the Royal Navy, like the Army, will rely on Royal Air Force land-based aircraft to support it....

The Army

5 The Army will continue to provide the major British contribution to NATO.

6 The size of the Army outside Europe will be gradually reduced. All our troops will leave South Arabia in January 1968; the increase in the garrison stationed in the Persian Gulf to meet our remaining obligations will be small. We are reducing the Cyprus garrison this year. In Malta, a programme of reductions will be completed by the end of 1971. In the Far East, the main reductions will be made in Malaysia and Singapore; we shall maintain the garrison in Hong Kong. From early 1968, the Strategic Reserve will be strengthened by a further infantry brigade....

Royal Air Force

9   The basic role of the Royal Air Force will remain as described in the Statements on the Defence Estimates 1966 (Cmnd 2901) and 1967 (Cmnd 3203); but the size of the front line will be reduced. More aircraft will be concentrated in Britain; the increased mobility, range and performance of the new aircraft make this possible. The reductions up to 1971 will occur mainly in the Far East, Aden and Malta; four squadrons of aircraft will be moved from Aden to the Persian Gulf and one from Germany to this country. . . .

Reductions in research and development programme

14   We have also reviewed the defence research and development programme. A cut of about £30m is to be made in the planned level of expenditure for 1970–1; it will affect development projects as well as research done in Government establishments and in industry, and will free scientists, technicians and other resources for civil work.

Service manpower

15   We intend that, by April 1971, the active strengths of the forces (UK uniformed personnel) shall fall by about 37,000 as follows:

	April 1967 (actual)	April 1971 (estimated)
Royal Navy	97,050	88,400
Army	196,200	181,200
Royal Air Force	124,110	110,500
Total	417,360	380,100

We are planning that they shall fall further in the years beyond 1971; we foresee a total drop of about 75,000 in present strengths by the time that we have finally withdrawn from Malaysia and Singapore in the mid-1970s.

V   Cost

2   As a result of the plans in this Statement, we expect to stay below the target of £2,000m a year from now on, even with transitional

expenditure on redeployment and compensation terms. The defence budget for 1970–1 should be of the order of £1,900m–£200m below the estimated level of £2,100m quoted above. By the mid-1970s, we foresee a budget of about £1,800m – a reduction of some £300m on that forecast last year. (The figures of £1,900m and £1,800m expressed at 1967 prices would be £2,200m and £2,100m respectively.) ...

VI Conclusion

2 Substantial savings will be made in the demands of defence on the nation's manpower and financial resources. More of our forces will be based in Britain. We plan no major change in the size of our contribution to NATO. The savings will be chiefly obtained from a significant reduction in our military presence outside Europe, and from some changes in its deployment.

Appendix IV
United Kingdom Defence Expenditure, 1948–1979

Year	Defence expenditure (£m) Current prices	Defence expenditure (£m) Constant prices (1970 = 100)	Defence as % of GNP	Manpower in services (000s)
1948	740	1737	7.1	847
1949	770	1754	6.5	770
1950	820	1814	6.6	690
1951	1090	2211	7.9	827
1952	1450	2690	9.8	827
1953	1540	2775	9.7	865
1954	1551	2745	9.2	839
1955	1523	2581	7.9	803
1956	1625	2621	7.8	761
1957	1551	2416	6.9	702
1958	1541	2328	6.7	615
1959	1561	2344	6.4	566
1960	1614	2398	6.3	519
1961	1725	2478	6.3	474
1962	1840	2358	6.4	442
1963	1892	2557	6.2	426
1964	1990	2605	5.9	423
1965	2105	2628	5.9	423
1966	2206	2651	5.8	417
1967	2410	2829	5.9	415
1968	2441	2733	5.6	399

Appendix IV

Year	Defence expenditure (£m) Current prices	Defence expenditure (£m) Constant prices (1970 = 100)	Defence as % of GNP	Manpower in services (000s)
1969	2295	2439	4.9	380
1970	2462	2462	4.8	378
1971	2777	2538	4.8	368
1972	3071	2618	4.8	371
1973	3470	2711	4.7	361
1974	4085	2751	4.9	345
1975	5164	2799	4.9	338
1976	6207	2888	4.9	336
1977	6859	2754	4.8	330
1978	7493	2768	4.6	321
1979	8149	2638	–	315

The constant price figures are based on the retail price index. Since there is a lack of a satisfactory price index for defence spending, the real expenditure figures should be treated as boundaries of magnitude.

Source: Keith Hartley, 'Defence with less money? The British experience', in Gwyn Harries-Jenkins (ed.), *Armed Forces and the Welfare Societies: Challenges in the 1980s* (London, 1982), p. 11. Reproduced by kind permission of Dr Hartley.

Appendix V
The United Kingdom Defence Programme: the Way Forward, 1981

1   The first duty of any British Government is to safeguard our people in peace and freedom. In today's world that cannot be done without a major defence effort. The international scene is in several areas unsettled and even turbulent. Soviet military power, already massive, continues to grow in size, quality and reach, and the Soviet leaders continue to demonstrate their readiness to use it brutally. The North Atlantic Alliance remains vital to us, and neither its strength nor its cohesion can be maintained without our crucial contribution. This is at the top of the Government's priorities.

2   Our policy is translated into practice initially through decisions on resources. Britain already spends 5.2 per cent of its gross domestic product on defence – one of the highest figures anywhere in the Alliance, even though we are not among the wealthiest members and continue to face sharp economic difficulties. The Government attaches such importance to its security responsibilities within the Alliance that defence expenditure is already 8 per cent higher in real terms than three years ago. It was announced in March, and has recently been reaffirmed, that the defence budget for the next two years (1982/3 and 1983/4) will reflect further annual growth at 3 per cent, in full implementation of the NATO aim. The Government has now firmly decided to plan to implement the aim in full for a further two years – 1984/5 and 1985/6 – and the programme will be shaped accordingly.

London, HMSO, Cmnd 8288, June 1981. Reproduced by kind permission of the Controller of HM Stationery Office.

The need for change

3   The Government's appraisal of the defence programme therefore in no way rests on a desire to cut our defence effort. On the contrary, it reflects a firm resolve to establish how best to exploit a substantial increase, which will enable us to enhance our front-line capability in very many areas. Defence spending on the scale we have decided is a heavy burden on the British people, but one which in our judgement they are prepared to bear. It is then however all the more incumbent upon the Government to ensure that resources are spent to the very best effect in terms of security. It has become clear that meeting this responsibility in the future calls for change in the defence programme. There are two main reasons for this.

4   First, even the increased resources we plan to allocate cannot adequately fund all the force structures and all the plans for their improvement we now have. One reason (not peculiar to Britain) is cost growth, especially in equipment.

5   The second reason for change, partly related to the first, concerns balance within the programme. Technological advance is sharply changing the defence environment. The fast-growing power of modern weapons to find targets accurately and hit them hard at long ranges is increasing the vulnerability of major platforms such as aircraft and surface ships. To meet this, and indeed to exploit it, the balance of our investment between platforms and weapons needs to be altered so as to maximise real combat capability....

Britain's defence roles

7   We have now four main roles: an independent element of strategic and theatre nuclear forces committed to the Alliance; the direct defence of the United Kingdom homeland; a major land and air contribution on the European mainland; and a major maritime effort in the Eastern Atlantic and Channel. We also commit home-based forces to the Alliance for specialist reinforcement contingencies, particularly on NATO's European flanks. Finally, we exploit the flexibility of our forces beyond the NATO area so far as our resources permit, to meet both specific British responsibilities and the growing importance to the West of supporting our friends and contributing to world stability more widely....

Nuclear forces

9 We intend to maintain and modernise our present nuclear role in the Alliance. No other member could in practice replace us in this distinctive contribution. NATO collectively, and our main allies individually, have made clear that they place high value upon it.

10 We intend accordingly to proceed with our plans for Trident. Certain aspects of the programme are still being studied, but however these are resolved expenditure over the next few years will remain comparatively modest. Review of all the options confirms that Trident remains by far the best way – indeed the only cost-effective way – of modernising the crucial strategic element of our capability. In the Government's firm judgement, no alternative application of defence resources could approach this in real deterrent insurance. The operation of the strategic force will remain the Royal Navy's first and most vital task for Britain's security. . . .

The British contribution on the Continent of Europe

16 The Government has considered with especial care the future of the large proportion of our land and air forces we maintain permanently in the Federal Republic of Germany, backed by a very extensive commitment for rapid reinforcement from the United Kingdom in emergency. Despite all the financial pressures on our defence effort, the Government has decided that this contribution is so important to the Alliance's military posture and its political cohesion that it must be maintained. The Central Region is the Alliance's heartland in Europe; the forward defence of the Federal Republic is the forward defence of Britain itself; and the full fighting strength of First British Corps is needed to guard the vital 65-kilometre sector assigned to it. We will therefore stand by our Brussels Treaty commitment of land and air forces, and the figure of 55,000 troops which we have upheld under it for over 20 years now. . . .

Maritime tasks

21 As the Government's review work proceeded it became clear that the most complex and difficult issues concerned the future shape of

Britain's maritime contribution. That such a contribution must continue, and on a major scale, is not in question. The importance of maritime tasks to Alliance security, our special skills and immense experience, and our existing assets all ensure this; so does our position as NATO's major European maritime power, situated crucially close to the Soviet Navy's long exit route to the open Atlantic. But we have to think hard about how we can most cost-effectively shape our contribution for the future, with account taken both of resource constraints and of technological change. . . .

Beyond the NATO area

32   As the Alliance collectively has acknowledged, changes in many areas of the world, together with growing Soviet military reach and readiness to exploit it directly or indirectly, make it increasingly necessary for NATO members to look to Western security concerns over a wider field than before, and not to assume that these concerns can be limited by the boundaries of the Treaty area. . . .

34   The Royal Navy has a particularly valuable role. For example, since the conflict broke out last year between Iran and Iraq a maritime presence has been maintained continuously in the Indian Ocean, with warships on rotation supported by fleet auxiliaries. We intend to resume from 1982 onwards the practice of sending a substantial naval task group on long detachment for visits and exercises in the South Atlantic, Caribbean, Indian Ocean or further east. We intend to make particular use of the new carriers, with Sea Harriers and helicopters, in out-of-area deployment. We will coordinate all these deployments and exercises as fruitfully as possible with the United States and other allies, as well as with local countries with whom we have close defence relations. . . .

36   Our forces will also continue as necessary to sustain specific British responsibilities overseas, for example in Gibraltar, Cyprus, Belize and the Falkland Islands. The Hong Kong garrison will be expanded by one infantry battalion in accordance with our agreement with the Hong Kong Government. . . .

Service manpower

Royal Navy numbers required will be reduced by between about 8,000 to 10,000 by 1986, partly through the surface fleet contraction and partly through cutting out posts and establishments ashore and undertaking more training afloat. Over the same period Army numbers will be reduced by up to about 7,000 and Royal Air Force numbers by about 2,500. All these reductions will be made so far as possible through natural wastage and careful control of recruitment rates. . . .

The way forward

47 In its review work the Government has confronted complex choices, with no easy or painless solutions available. To go on simply as before, or with all plans and aspirations unabated, is not an option; change is necessary. The Government has taken hard decisions. These reflect our resolve to give defence the resources Britain's security demands; but equal resolve to see that these resources, which the nation cannot spare without much penalty elsewhere, are put to work in accordance with realistic, unsentimental and up-to-date judgement of what will be most relevant and effective in future years.

Outline Chronology

1945

8 May — Defeat of Germany. Britain begins to demobilize her armed services, then standing at about 5 million men.

July — General Election results in Labour victory; Clement Attlee, Prime Minister.

15 August — Japan's surrender ends war in Asia.

1946

12 November — Britain introduces National Service: at first for 18 months but it is increased to two years in 1950.

1947

1 January — The Ministry of Defence Act attempts to centralize Britain's defence organization under a Minister of Defence, but the measure proves to be inadequate: the Minister has no real powers. Gen 163 Cabinet Committee orders production of independent British atomic bomb after the United States withdraws nuclear cooperation with the United Kingdom.

21 February — Britain notifies United States that she can no longer aid Greece and Turkey.

15 August — Britain grants independence to India and Pakistan.

1948

17 March — Brussels collective security treaty signed by Britain, France, Belgium, The Netherlands and Luxembourg.

April — Britain withdraws from Palestine mandate.

1949

4 April — North Atlantic Treaty signed by five Brussels treaty powers, the United States, Canada, Iceland, Norway, Denmark, Italy, Portugal who agree to aid each other in the event of an attack. Greece and Turkey join in 1951.

1950

25 June — North Korean invasion of South Korea: in July Britain sends naval forces and a small army contingent of two battalions to assist the United Nations' effort in South Korea.

12 September — Labour government announces £3,600 million rearmament programme over next three years.

1951

29 January — Labour government increases rearmament programme expenditure to £4,700 million over next three years. Mussadiq nationalizes the British owned Anglo-Iranian oil company. This precipitates a crisis which was not settled until 1953, when Mussadiq overthrown.

9 October — Egyptian government repudiates Anglo-Egyptian treaty of 1936 and campaign of violence begins against British base at Suez.

26 October — General Election returns Conservatives to power, with Winston Churchill as Prime Minister. Financial crisis in 1951/2 leads this government to reduce Labour's rearmament programme.

1952	Mau Mau uprising in Kenya.
July	The Cabinet approves Global Strategy Paper, produced by the Chiefs of Staff as basis for defence policy for rest of decade, and calling for more reliance in future on Britain's nuclear deterrent. Army and navy still to have a major role in any global conventional war.
3 October	British atomic bomb tested at Monte Bello Island.
1954	
27 July	Anglo-Egyptian treaty signed: Britain to withdraw from Suez base by 1956.
8 September	South East Asia Treaty Organization (SEATO) set up consisting of Great Britain, France, the United States, Australia, New Zealand, Pakistan, Thailand and the Philippines.
3 October	London Nine-Power Agreement of the six former European Defence Community powers, Britain, the United States and Canada paves the way for West Germany's entry into NATO and the Brussels Pact (now Western European Union). Anthony Eden pledges that Britain will retain her four divisions and a Tactical Air Force in West Germany indefinitely.
1955	
April	Anthony Eden replaces Winston Churchill as Prime Minister. Neither his efforts to reduce defence expenditure nor those to strengthen the powers of the Minister of Defence very successful.
4 April	Britain joins Central Treaty Organization (Baghdad Pact) with Turkey and Iraq. Iran and Pakistan join later in the year.
November	State of emergency declared in Cyprus.

1956

November — Anglo-French expedition to Suez.

1957

10 January — Harold Macmillan replaces Eden as Prime Minister. Selwyn Lloyd Minister of Defence with mandate to make sweeping reductions in British armed services. His White Paper, *Outline of Future Policy* emphasizes nuclear deterrence and abolishes national service by 1960. Cuts also in size of navy and RAF. Britain agrees to defend independent Malaya. BAOR reduced from 77,000 to 64,000 men (in 1959 further reduced to 55,000 men).

15 May — Britain test explodes hydrogen bomb.

1958

July — Coup in Iraq results in Iraq's exit from Baghdad Pact. British troops sent to defend Jordan.

1959

July — Earl Mountbatten of Burma becomes Chief of Defence Staff.

1960

June — Britain purchases Skybolt air-to-ground missile from United States after cancellation of Blue Streak.

1961

July — British task force sent to defend Kuwait from threatened Iraqi invasion.

1962

18–21 December — Macmillan secures submarine-launched Polaris missiles from United States in place of cancelled Skybolt.

1963

18 January	Aden accedes to South Arabian Federation and Arab nationalists begin campaign against British presence.
20 January	Indonesia announces policy of 'confrontation' with new Federation of Malaysia. Indonesian guerrilla activities in Malaysia lead to steady reinforcement of British forces.

1964

October	Harold Wilson's Labour government enters office.

1967

18 July	Labour government's Supplementary Defence White Paper announces that British forces will be withdrawn from Singapore and Malaysia by mid-1970s.

1968

16 January	Harold Wilson announces withdrawal of British forces from Far East and Persian Gulf by 1971.

1969

Violence erupts in Northern Ireland. British troops sent in to take over police duties.

1970

Conservative election victory. Edward Heath Prime Minister. House of Commons Defence and External Affairs Sub-committee set up.

1972

1 April	Procurement Executive set up in Ministry of Defence.

1974

February	Harold Wilson's second Labour government.
December	Roy Mason, the Defence Secretary, introduces Labour's Defence Review for the next ten years.

1979

Labour agrees to spend additional 3 per cent per

	annum improving her NATO forces for five years.
May	Conservatives returned to office under Margaret Thatcher.
1980	
July	Francis Pym, the Defence Secretary announces that Trident is to be purchased from United States to replace Polaris in 1980s.
1981	
June	John Nott's Defence Review, *The Way Forward*, calls for drastic cuts in Britain's surface fleet.
1982	
April–June	The Falklands War.

Further Reading

While there are a large number of substantive works on British defence policy in this period, much useful information about this subject can be obtained from the numerous collections of essays which have appeared in recent years. Many of these contain updated accounts of recent trends in British defence policy often by the authors of the earlier books. Of special interest are the following: John Baylis (ed.) *British Defence Policy in a Changing World* (London, 1977), a set of articles by some of the leading British academic writers on both the historical and contemporary aspects of Britain and her defences, dealing with relations with the United States and NATO, British strategic thought, the influence of public opinion etc.; John Baylis (ed.) *Alternative Approaches to British Defence Policy* (London, 1983), where academics and military leaders have joined together to examine the future prospects for Britain's defences in the 1980s; Gregory Frank, Mark Imber and John Simpson (eds) *Perspectives upon British Defence Policy 1945–70* (Proceedings of a Ministry of Defence Conference held at Winchester in April 1975), perhaps somewhat dated now but these essays by prominent civil servants, naval officers and scholars discuss British defence policy, past and present, from the perspective of the mid-1970s; and John Roper (ed.) *The Future of British Defence Policy* (London, 1985), a product of a Chatham House conference in December 1985 about alternative defence strategies for the 1990s.

Individual essays of interest to this theme include Keith Hartley 'Defence with less money? The British experience' in Gwyn Harries-Jenkins (ed.) *Armed Forces and the Welfare Societies: Challenges in the 1980s* (London, 1982) which contains some useful statistics pertaining to the British economy and its defence and considers the options available to British policy-makers in the future; L. W. Martin, *British Defence Policy:*

the Long Recessional (London, 1969), an earlier discussion of the changes that took place in Britain's defences down to 1968; John Keegan, 'Western Europe and its armies, 1945–1985' and Roger Beaumont, 'The British armed forces since 1945' in L. H. Gann (ed.) *The Defence of Western Europe* (London, 1987) and John Baylis '"Greenwoodery" and British defence policy', in *International Affairs*, vol. 62, no. 3 (summer, 1986), pp. 443–57, which addressed the major issues in the debate between the orthodox views of Britain's defence policy and David Greenwood.

Of the major books and monographs which have been published in recent years on this subject I have found the following most useful: Dan Smith, *The Defence of the Realm in the 1980s* (London, 1980), a critical and well-written account of British defence policy and of the stark choices which may have to be faced by defence planners if there is no long-term improvement in Britain's economic performance; F. A. Johnson, *Defence by Ministry: the British Ministry of Defence, 1944–1974* (London, 1980), which is a reliable discussion of the organizational and administrative changes which have taken place within the British defence establishment since the end of the Second World War; Philip Darby, *British Defence Policy East of Suez, 1947–1968* (Oxford, 1973), a well-researched and thoughtful survey of the process by which Britain finally abandoned her imperial pretention in 1968: I found this a most useful source of information; C. J. Bartlett, *The Long Retreat: a Short History of British Defence Policy, 1945–1970* (London, 1972), a clear, if rather dated, survey of the subject down to 1970; and Michael Chichester and John Wilkinson, *The Uncertain Ally* (London, 1982), which rehearses the arguments of the school which believes that Britain has been in continuous decline since 1945. Of this school also are the earlier works, which have been somewhat overtaken in some aspects by more recent studies, by R. N. Rosecrance, *British Strategy in the Nuclear Epoch* (New York, 1968) and W. P. Snyder *The Politics of British Defence Policy 1945–1962* (Columbus, Ohio, 1964).

On the nuclear issue in particular and Anglo-American strategic relations in general are A. J. R. Groom, *British Thinking about Nuclear Weapons* (London, 1974), a lengthy but thorough account of all aspects of Britain's post-1945 nuclear weapons policy; John Simpson, *The Independent Nuclear State: the United States, Britain and the Military Atom*, 2nd edn (London, 1986) and John Baylis, *Anglo-American Defence Relations, 1939–80* (London, 1980), a clear and interesting overview of the Anglo-American nuclear relationship; Margaret Gowing, *Independence and Deterrence: Britain and Atomic Energy, 1945–1952*, 2 vols (London, 1974), the official history of Britain's road to an independent nuclear deterrent, using classified material which is still closed to other scholars; J. P. C. Freeman, *Britain's Nuclear Arms Control Policy in the Context of Anglo-American Relations* (London, 1986); based on a PhD thesis, this book deals with Britain's policy towards the Partial Test Ban Treaty of 1963 and the Non-Proliferation Treaty of 1968, the last occasion when Britain was able to exert any influence over the arms control process; Lawrence Freedman, *The Evolution of Nuclear Strategy* (London, 1983) which, while dealing mainly with American strategic thought, contains some interesting insights into British thinking about nuclear weapons; and, more specifically, Lawrence Freedman, *Britain and Nuclear Weapons* (London, 1980).

Finally, in my view the best of the many accounts of the Falklands War are those by Max Hastings and Simon Jenkins, *The Battle for the Falklands* (London, 1983), which deals thoroughly with both the military and diplomatic events, and the excellent concise analysis by Lawrence Freedman, *Britain and the Falklands War* (Oxford, 1988).

Index

Acland, Sir Anthony 118
Aden 68, 78, 89, 94–5
Admiralty, the First Lord of the 5–6, 37–8, 57, 88
Afghanistan 109
Africa 22, 29, 70, 83, 86, 126
Air, Secretary of State for 5–6, 37
Alexander, A. V. 38
Algeria 60, 126
Anti-Ballistic Missile Treaty (ABM) 107
Argentina 9, 111, 115–20
Attlee, Clement 10, 15, 21, 23, 25–6, 28–9, 37–8, 43–4
Australia 31, 42, 55, 62, 68, 103, 107, 118
Austria 39
Austria-Hungary 16

Balfour, Arthur 2, 37
Baruch Plan 25
Baylis, John 125
Belgium 32
Belize 95, 107–8
Berlin 32–3, 52, 85
Bermuda Conference, March 1957 71
Bevan, Aneurin 43–4, 84
Bevin, Ernest 21, 27–8, 33, 52
Blackett, Professor 8
Blue Steak 69, 71–2
Blue Steel 69, 72

Boer War 15, 37
Bridges, Lord 38
British Army 5, 15–19, 26, 29, 43, 47, 51, 57, 64, 68, 70, 88, 99–101, 105–6, 115, 128
British Army of the Rhine (BAOR) 46, 68, 76–7, 84, 86, 91, 97, 99, 101, 103, 105, 109, 111, 114
British Empire 14–17, 23, 28, 126
British Expeditionary Force (BEF) 15–17, 19, 34
Buchan, Alistair 8
Butler, R. A. 56

Cabinet 1, 4, 7, 9, 11, 26, 29, 34, 38, 51, 56, 60, 66, 71, 80, 85–6, 89–90, 117–20
Callaghan, James 99, 108–9, 112, 116
Campaign for Nuclear Disarmament (CND) 10, 47, 84–5, 113–14
Canada 23–5, 33, 122
Canberra Fighter Bomber 36, 54, 74, 91–2, 118, 120
Carrington, Lord 103, 118
Carter, President James 108, 113
Central Defence Scientific Staff 6
Central Treaty Organisation (CENTO) or Baghdad Pact 54, 55, 70, 103
Centurion Tank 45, 91

Index

Ceylon (Sri Lanka) 22, 28, 39, 70, 92
Chalfont, Lord 8
Chamberlain, Neville 3, 5, 8
Chancellor of the Exchequer 1, 6, 14, 21, 37, 43, 56, 58, 63, 66, 88, 90
Chevaline Project 107, 110
Chichester, M. 125
Chief of the Defence Staff 6, 67, 88
Chief of the Imperial General Staff 5, 15, 59
Chief Scientific Adviser 6, 67, 78, 89
Chiefs of Staff, British 4–6, 9, 26, 29, 37–8, 54, 60–1, 63, 66–7, 78, 88, 106, 109
Chieftain Tank 91, 109, 129
China 18, 42–3, 52, 59, 102, 115
Churchill, Winston 3–4, 10, 14, 22–3, 37–8, 44, 56
Cold War 20–1, 32, 39, 58
Committee of Imperial Defence (CID) 37–8
Commonwealth, the 11, 42, 66, 68, 86–7, 94, 96
Communism 20, 22, 27–8, 31–2, 39, 42, 49, 55, 80
Congress, United States 3–4, 18, 23, 25–6, 28, 33, 71
Conservative Party 3, 10, 18, 92
Cooper, Sir Frank 118
Cruise Missiles 112–13
Cuban Missile Crisis, 1962 88
Cyprus 53–4, 60–1, 70, 78–9, 89, 107–8
Czechoslovakia 55, 97

Dalton, Hugh 21
Defence Committee, Cabinet 1, 34, 38, 89
Defence Council 6, 88
Defence and External Affairs Sub-Committee (House of Commons) 3, 122
Defence Operational Analysis Establishment 6

Defence and Overseas Policy Committee (Cabinet) 1, 4, 89, 118
Defence Research Policy Committee 38, 51
Defence Review, 1974 104–5
Defence Review, 1981 115
Defence, Secretary of State for 1, 6–7, 9, 88, 128
Defence White Paper, 1957 67–70, 72, 79–80, 82–3, 127
De Gaulle, General 76, 96, 101
Dickens, Sir William 59
Diego Garcia 103, 107–8
Divine, David 8
Douglas-Home, Charles 8
Dulles, John Foster 59, 62
Dunkirk, Treaty of, 1947 32

Eden, Anthony 10, 12, 53, 56, 58–9, 61–3, 65–6
Egypt 22, 29–32, 41, 53, 55, 58–64, 79
Egypt Committee, 1956 59–60
Eisenhower, Dwight D. 12, 47, 49, 51–2, 62–4, 71–2, 75, 80
Elbe River 50
Endurance, HMS 11, 117
Ethiopia 18
European Defence Community (EDC) 49–50, 56
European Economic Community (EEC) 82, 96, 101, 110, 119

Falklands Islands 95, 107–8, 115–21, 128
Falklands War, 1982 9, 11–13, 111–12, 116–21, 128
Far East 15, 18–20, 28–9, 31, 39, 42, 54, 55, 59, 69, 78, 86–7, 89, 126
Fieldhouse, Admiral Sir John 118
First World War 3, 6, 16–18, 21, 37
Fisher, Admiral Sir John 15
Foot, Michael 10
Foreign Office 4, 7, 11–12, 21, 116
Foreign Secretary 1, 11, 37, 58–9, 84
France 15–16, 18–19, 22, 32, 34,

40, 48–50, 55–6, 59–63, 75–7, 82–3, 92–3, 101, 107, 130
Freedman, Lawrence 12, 130
Fuchs, Klaus 26
Fuller, Major-General J. F. C. 17

Gaitskell, Hugh 43, 85
Galtieri, General Leopoldo 117, 120
Germany 3, 15–19, 22–4, 26–9, 32–6, 39, 42, 44, 48–51, 55–6, 74, 77, 84, 90, 93, 105, 113, 124
Gibraltar 95, 107–8, 119
Global Strategy Paper, 1952 45–7
Gorbachev, Mikhail 130
Greece 22, 23, 28, 39, 54, 79
Greenwood, David 125, 128

Haig, Alexander 119–20
Haldane, Richard Burdon 15
Healey, Denis 7, 88–9, 91–2, 97
Heath, Edward 10, 99, 101–6, 110, 112
Heseltine, Michael 122, 128
Hitler, Adolf 18–19
Home, Lord 59
Hong Kong 22, 46, 51, 55, 86, 95, 107, 115
Hore-Belisha, Leslie 7–8
House of Commons 2–3, 21, 117
Howard, Sir Michael 8
Hyde Park Agreement, 1944 24–5

Iceland 33, 105
India 14, 23, 28–9, 39, 102, 126
Indo-China 22, 49, 126
Indonesia 22, 79, 82, 89, 94, 98, 126
International Institute of Strategic Studies 8
Iran 23, 29, 53–4, 123, 129
Iraq 29–30, 54–5, 58, 78–9, 89, 98
Irish Republican Army (IRA) 100
Ismay, General Lord 38, 88
Israel 30, 55, 61–2, 94, 102
Italy 18, 22, 29, 33, 39, 93, 119, 123

Jacob, General Sir Ian 38, 88
Jaguar Ground Attack Fighter 101, 124

Japan 16, 18–19, 24, 27, 42, 44–5, 87, 128
Johnson, President Lyndon B. 86
Joint Chiefs of Staff (United States) 3, 4
Jordan 29–31, 55, 58, 78–9

Kennedy, President John F. 75–8, 86, 88
Kenya 51–2, 70, 79
King, Mackenzie 25
Korean War 40–4, 48, 51–2, 63, 71
Khrushchev, Nikita 51–2, 77, 85
Kuwait 79

Labour Party 3, 10, 14, 21, 47, 84–5, 93, 98, 104–5, 114, 126
Lambe, Sir Charles 78
Lewin, Sir Terence 118
Libya 22, 29, 31, 39, 61
Liddell Hart, Sir Basil 7–8
Lincoln Bomber 30
Lloyd, Selwyn 57–9
Locarno Pact 17
Luce, Admiral Sir David 92
Luxembourg 32

Macleod, Ian 70
McMahon Act 25
Macmillan, Harold 5, 10, 58, 63, 65–7, 71–2, 74–7, 126
McNamara, Robert S. 75, 97
Main Battle Tank (MBT) 109
Malaya (Malaysia) 20, 22, 31–2, 39, 51, 55, 68, 79, 86, 94–5, 103
Maldives 70
Malta 61
Manchuria 18, 43
Manhattan Project 23–6
Marshall Plan, 1948 28, 44
Martin, Lawrence 8
Mason, Roy 104, 107
Mayhew, Christopher 92
Mediterranean 27, 29, 32, 54, 60, 78, 105–6
Menendez, General M. 121

Index

Middle East 16, 20, 22, 27–31, 33, 39, 51–5, 58–9, 66, 69–70, 78, 83, 86, 89, 102, 129
Ministerial Production Committee 38
Minuteman Intercontinental Ballistic Missile 75
Monckton, Sir Walter 58, 60
Monte Bello Island Nuclear Tests 45, 71
Morley, John 4
Morrison, Herbert 52
Mountbatten, Lord 5–6, 59, 67, 78, 88
Mulley, Frederick 107
Mussadiq 52–3
Mussolini, Benito 58

Nassau Conference, 1962 75–6, 85
Nasser, Colonel Gamel Abdel 55, 58–60, 62, 66
Netherlands, The 22, 32, 102, 126
New Zealand 31, 42, 55, 62, 68, 103, 107
Nixon, President Richard M. 102
North Atlantic Treaty Organization (NATO) 31–3, 41–2, 46, 48–50, 56, 75–7, 80, 82, 84–5, 89, 96–8, 103, 105, 107–8, 110–12, 114–15, 122–4, 126, 130
North Sea 16, 105, 108
Northern Ireland 13, 99, 101, 115–16
Nott, John 114–15, 117–18

Organization of Arab Petroleum Exporting Countries (OPEC) 102
Ottoman Empire 16

Pakistan 39, 54–5, 102
Palestine 22, 29–30
Parkinson, Cecil 118
Parliament 2–4, 26, 51, 107
Pearl Harbor 19
Persian Gulf 11, 29, 46, 59, 68, 78, 80, 82, 86, 94–5, 98, 112, 128
Philippines 42, 55

Polaris 10, 74–6, 80, 85–6, 91, 106, 113, 129
Pompidou, President Georges 101
Poseidon 106
Post, Colonel 7
Potsdam Conference, 1945 22
Prime Minister 1–2, 5–7, 9, 24, 37, 56, 65–6, 104, 106, 108, 112, 117
Procurement Executive 6–7
Public Accounts Committee (House of Commons) 3
Pym, Francis 112, 114, 118–19

Quebec Agreement, 1943 24, 25

Reagan, President Ronald 113, 130
Rhine, River 33, 48
Rhodesia (Zimbabwe) 94, 115
Roberts, Goronwy 97
Roosevelt, President Franklin Delano 23–4
Royal Air Force 3, 5, 17, 19, 32–3, 45, 47, 51, 57, 68, 70, 75, 88, 92, 95, 101, 105–6, 109, 128
Royal Navy 3, 5, 15, 17–19, 35, 47, 51, 57, 68, 88, 91–2, 95, 101, 103, 105–6, 111–12, 114–15, 118, 122, 128
Russia 15–17

Salisbury, Lord 59
Sandys, Duncan 5–7, 11, 38, 65–70, 72, 77, 82–3, 98, 126
Saudi Arabia 79
Schuman, Robert 49
Sea Harrier (VTOL) Jets 103, 119–21
Second World War 10, 20–1, 30, 35, 39, 44–5, 68, 73, 102, 125
Select Committee on Estimates (House of Commons) 3
Shinwell, Emmanuel 38
Singapore 46, 55, 68, 70, 79, 89, 95, 103, 197
Skybolt 72, 74–6, 80
Slessor, Sir John, Marshal of the Royal Air Force 45–6, 50
Smith, Dan 104

Index

Smith, Ian 94, 115
South Africa 15, 31, 62, 78, 87, 103, 107
South East Asia Security Organization (SEATO) 55, 70
South Georgia 11, 116–17, 119–20
Soviet Union 18–23, 25–8, 30, 32–5, 42, 46, 48, 50–1, 53–5, 63, 70, 72, 75, 84–6, 89–90, 97, 102, 107–8, 110, 112, 129–30
Spain 116
Speed, Keith 115
Stalin, J. V. 51
Strategic Arms Limitation Talks (SALT) 97, 107
Suez Canal 29–30, 46, 53, 59–63
Suez Crisis, 1956 9, 11–13, 58–63, 65–6, 68, 70, 80, 83, 121, 127
Suez Role, East of 9–11, 68, 74, 78, 80–2, 86–7, 91, 93, 95, 97–8, 101, 103–4, 126–7
Supreme Allied Commander, Europe (SACEUR) 107
Supreme Headquarters Allied Powers in Europe (SHAPE) 96–7
Syria 63

Tanganyika (Tanzania) 79
Templar, Field Marshal Sir Gerald 5, 59
Territorial Army 15, 104, 124
Test Ban Treaty, 1963 88
Thailand 55
Thatcher, Margaret 10–11, 111–15, 118, 121
Thorneycroft, Peter 80, 88, 90
Tornado Multi-Role Combat Aircraft 93, 124
Treasury 8, 19, 38–9, 51, 74, 77, 130

Trenchard, Lord 5
Trident 10, 113–14, 129
Trieste 51
Trincomalee 28, 70, 92
Truman, President Harry S. 23, 28, 42–3, 45–6
TSR2 Strike and Reconnaissance Aircraft 72–4, 91
Turkey 53–4, 79

Uganda 79
United Nations Organization (UN) 21–2, 41–2, 62–3, 116, 119
United States of America 3–4, 8–12, 18–21, 23–8, 31–4, 39, 42, 44, 46, 48–55, 63, 65–6, 70–7, 80, 83, 85–7, 96, 101, 103, 106–8, 111–14, 120, 122, 129–30

V-Bombers 36, 44–5, 58, 68–9, 72, 74, 101
Vietnam War 12, 88, 96, 102, 108

War Office 15, 18, 57
War, Secretary of State for 5–6, 15, 37
Watkinson, Harold 72, 74, 77–80
West Indies 15
Western Europe 9–10, 20, 26–8, 32–3, 41–2, 48–50, 101–2, 111–12, 124, 128
Whitelaw, William 118
Wilkinson, J. 125
Wilson, Harold 8, 10, 82, 85–6, 88–9, 91, 95, 97–9, 103–4, 106–8, 126–7

Younger, George 122, 123

Zuckerman, Solly 8, 78